A GIFT FOR: _____

FROM: _____

Wisdom is supreme; therefore get wisdom.
   Though it cost all you have, get understanding.

                                    —Proverbs 4:7

Daily Inspiration for Students
from the New International Version
Copyright © 2005 by The Zondervan Corporation
ISBN-10: 0-310-81004-3
ISBN-13: 978-0-310-81004-9

Requests for information should be addressed to:
Inspirio, The gift group of Zondervan
Grand Rapids, Michigan 49530
http://www.inspiriogifts.com

Compiler: June Gunden / Peachtree Editorial Services
Project Manager: Tom Dean
Design Manager: Val Buick
Cover Design: Michael J. Williams
Interior Design: Melissa Elenbaas
Cover Photo: Ryuhei Shindo / Photonica

Printed in the United States of America

05 06 07 /OPM/ 4 3 2 1

DAILY
INSPIRATION
for students

from the New International Version

inspirio™

CONTENTS

Week 1: The Source of Knowledge

Week 2: The Importance of Learning

Week 3: Having a Good Attitude

Week 4: Resisting Temptation

Week 5: Talents and Gifts

Week 6: The Importance of Hard Work

Week 7: Making Choices

Week 8: Accepting the Consequences of Our Choices

Week 9: Avoiding Bad Habits

Week 10: Becoming Wise

Week 11: Being Discerning

Week 12: Choosing Good Friends

Week 13: Antidote for Worry

Week 14: A Clear Focus

Week 15: Being Honest

Week 16: Concern for the Future

Week 17: Overcoming Fear

Week 18: Resisting Cheating

Week 19: The Value of Instruction

Week 20: Being a True Friend

Week 21: The Importance of Listening

Week 22: Being Disciplined

Week 23: Staying Positive

Week 24: Not Giving Up

Week 25: Avoiding Fights and Arguments

Week 26: Guarding Your Health

Week 27: Listening to Advice

Week 28: Controlling Anger

Week 29: A Good Reputation

Week 30: The Pitfalls of Gossip

Week 31: The Pressures of Conformity

Week 32: The Need for Courage

Week 33: Resisting Laziness

Week 34: Watching Your Temper

Week 35: Being Obedient

Week 36: Dealing with Anxiety

Week 37: Seeking Direction

Week 38: Facing Rejection

Week 39: The Danger of Pride

Week 40: Getting Your Rest

Week 41: Developing Healthy Relationships

Week 42: Respecting Those in Authority

Week 43: Struggling with Doubt

Week 44: Staying Pure in an Evil Environment

Week 45: Finding Success

Week 46: Taking Advice

Week 47: Guarding Against Peer Pressure

Week 48: Asking God for Help

Week 49: Renewing Your Spirit

Week 50: Using Time Well

Week 51: Strength from God

Week 52: The Value of Wisdom

INTRODUCTION

The education process requires you, the student, to face schedules and challenges that are sure to cause you stress and anxiety at one time or another. God's Word speaks to these and other special needs you may have, and it gives perspective to the process of learning.

The Bible teaches us that everything we can possibly learn originates with God, and the revelation of all of our knowledge comes to us as his gift. Not only is God the source of all wisdom and learning, he is also the giver of all good gifts to us, including our minds. It is important that we reverence (the NIV uses the word "fear") him as a first step in learning.

You will likely face unique challenges in areas such as relationships, time-management, health, and attitudes during your years of formal education. We have chosen Scriptures that speak to these topics with the hope that they will provide you with guidance, blessing, and strength during these important years.

THE SOURCE OF KNOWLEDGE

Monday

The fear of the LORD is the beginning of
    knowledge,
but fools despise wisdom and discipline.

—**Proverbs 1:7**

The eyes of the LORD keep watch over
knowledge,
but he frustrates the words of the unfaithful.

—**Proverbs 22:12**

DANIEL PRAYED:
"Praise be to the name of God for ever and
ever;
    wisdom and power are his.
He changes times and seasons;
he sets up kings and deposes them.
He gives wisdom to the wise
    and knowledge to the discerning.
He reveals deep and hidden things;
he knows what lies in darkness,
and light dwells with him."

—**Daniel 2:20–22**

THE SOURCE OF KNOWLEDGE

Tuesday

Teach me, O LORD, to follow your decrees;
    then I will keep them to the end.
Give me understanding, and I will keep your law
    and obey it with all my heart.
Direct me in the path of your commands,
    for there I find delight.
Turn my heart toward your statutes
    and not toward selfish gain.
Turn my eyes away from worthless things;
    preserve my life according to your word.
Fulfill your promise to your servant,
    so that you may be feared.
Take away the disgrace I dread,
    for your laws are good.
How I long for your precepts!
    Preserve my life in your righteousness.

Do good to your servant
    according to your word, O LORD.
Teach me knowledge and good judgment,
    for I believe in your commands.

—Psalm 119:33–40, 65–66

THE SOURCE OF KNOWLEDGE

Wednesday

The fear of the LORD is the beginning of wisdom;
all who follow his precepts have good
understanding.
To him belongs eternal praise.

—**Psalm 111:10**

The heavens declare the glory of God;
 the skies proclaim the work of his hands.
Day after day they pour forth speech;
 night after night they display knowledge.
There is no speech or language
 where their voice is not heard.
Their voice goes out into all the earth,
 their words to the ends of the world.

—**Psalm 19:1–4**

Who has understood the mind of the LORD,
or instructed him as his counselor?
Whom did the LORD consult to enlighten him,
and who taught him the right way?
Who was it that taught him knowledge
or showed him the path of understanding?

—**Isaiah 40:13–14**

Thursday

PAUL WRITES:

"My purpose is that [the believers] may be encouraged in heart and united in love, so that they may have the full riches of complete understanding, in order that they may know the mystery of God, namely, Christ, in whom are hidden all the treasures of wisdom and knowledge."

—Colossians 2:2–3

O LORD, you have searched me
  and you know me.
You know when I sit and when I rise;
  you perceive my thoughts from afar.
You discern my going out and my lying down;
  you are familiar with all my ways.
Before a word is on my tongue
  you know it completely, O LORD.

You hem me in—behind and before;
you have laid your hand upon me.
Such knowledge is too wonderful for me,
too lofty for me to attain.

—Psalm 139:1–6

THE SOURCE OF KNOWLEDGE

Friday

JESUS SAID TO HIS DISCIPLES:
"The knowledge of the secrets of ... heaven has been given to you, but not to them. Whoever has will be given more.... Whoever does not have, even what he has will be taken from him. This is why I speak to them in parables:

'Though seeing, they do not see;
though hearing, they do not hear
or understand.

In *them is fulfilled the prophecy of Isaiah:*

"'You will be ever hearing but never understanding;
you will be ever seeing but never perceiving.
For this people's heart has become calloused;
they hardly hear with their ears,
and they have closed their eyes.
Otherwise they might see with their eyes,
hear with their ears....'
But blessed are your eyes because they see,
and your ears because they hear."

—**Matthew 13:11–16**

THE SOURCE OF KNOWLEDGE

Weekend

My son, if you accept my words
  and store up my commands within you,
turning your ear to wisdom
  and applying your heart to understanding,
and if you call out for insight
  and cry aloud for understanding,
and if you look for it as for silver
  and search for it as for hidden treasure,
then you will understand the fear of the LORD
  and find the knowledge of God.
For the LORD gives wisdom,
  and from his mouth come knowledge
and understanding.

—Proverbs 2:1–6

PAUL WRITES:
Since the day we heard about you, we have not
stopped praying for you and asking God to fill
you with the knowledge of his will through all
spiritual wisdom and understanding.

—Colossians 1:9

THE IMPORTANCE OF LEARNING

Monday

Wisdom is supreme; therefore get wisdom.
  Though it cost all you have, get understanding.
Esteem her, and she will exalt you;
  embrace her, and she will honor you.
She will set a garland of grace on your head
  and present you with a crown of splendor.

Listen, my son, accept what I say,
  and the years of your life will be many.
I guide you in the way of wisdom
  and lead you along straight paths.
When you walk, your steps will not be hampered;
  when you run, you will not stumble.

—Proverbs 4:7–12

Understanding is a fountain of life to those
who have it,
  but folly brings punishment to fools.

—Proverbs 16:22

THE IMPORTANCE OF LEARNING

Tuesday

Listen, my sons, to a father's instruction;
  pay attention and gain understanding.
I give you sound learning,
  so do not forsake my teaching.
When I was a boy in my father's house,
  still tender, and an only child of my mother,
he taught me and said,
  "Lay hold of my words with all your heart;
  keep my commands and you will live.
Get wisdom, get understanding;
  do not forget my words or swerve from them.
Do not forsake wisdom, and she will protect you;
  love her, and she will watch over you."

—Proverbs 4:1–6

PAUL WRITES:
I want to know Christ and the power of his resurrection and the fellowship of sharing in his sufferings, becoming like him in his death, and so, somehow, to attain to the resurrection from the dead.

—Philippians 3:10–11

THE IMPORTANCE OF LEARNING

Wednesday

Does not wisdom call out?
  Does not understanding raise her voice?
On the heights along the way,
  where the paths meet, she takes her stand;
beside the gates leading into the city,
  at the entrances, she cries aloud:
"You who are simple, gain prudence;
  you who are foolish, gain understanding.
Listen, for I have worthy things to say;
  I open my lips to speak what is right.
My mouth speaks what is true,
  for my lips detest wickedness.
All the words of my mouth are just;
  none of them is crooked or perverse.
To the discerning all of them are right;
  they are faultless to those who
have knowledge.
Choose my instruction instead of silver,
  knowledge rather than choice gold,
for wisdom is more precious than rubies,
  and nothing you desire can compare with her."

—**Proverbs 8:1–3, 5–11**

Thursday

It *is not good to have zeal without knowledge, nor to be hasty and miss the way.*

—Proverbs 19:2

PAUL WRITES:

Brothers, my heart's desire and prayer to God for the Israelites is that they may be saved. For I can testify about them that they are zealous for God, but their zeal is not based on knowledge.

—Romans 10:1–2

And this is my prayer: that your love may abound more and more in knowledge and depth of insight, so that you may be able to discern what is best and may be pure and blameless until the day of Christ, filled with the fruit of *righteousness that comes through Jesus Christ—to the glory and praise of God.*

—Philippians 1:9–11

THE IMPORTANCE OF LEARNING

Friday

The law of the LORD is perfect,
  reviving the soul.
The statutes of the LORD are trustworthy,
  making wise the simple.
The precepts of the LORD are right,
  giving joy to the heart.
The commands of the LORD are radiant,
  giving light to the eyes.
The fear of the LORD is pure,
  enduring forever.
The ordinances of the LORD are sure
  and altogether righteous.
They are more precious than gold,
  than much pure gold;
they are sweeter than honey,
  than honey from the comb.
By them is your servant warned;
  in keeping them there is great reward.

—Psalm 19:7–11

WEEK 2

THE IMPORTANCE OF LEARNING

Weekend

MOSES SAID TO THE ISRAELITES:
See, I have taught you decrees and laws as the LORD my God commanded me, so that you may follow them in the land you are entering to take possession of it. Observe them carefully, for this will show your wisdom and understanding to the nations, who will hear about all these decrees and say, "Surely this great nation is a wise and understanding people." What other nation is so great as to have their gods near them the way the LORD our God is near us whenever we pray to him? And what other nation is so great as to have such righteous decrees and laws as this body of laws I am setting before you today?

Only be careful, and watch yourselves closely so that you do not forget the things your eyes have seen or let them slip from your heart as long as you live. Teach them to your children and to their children after them.

—Deuteronomy 4:5–9

HAVING A GOOD ATTITUDE

Monday

JESUS SAID TO HIS DISCIPLES:
If you obey my commands, you will remain in my love, just as I have obeyed my Father's commands and remain in his love. I have told you this so that my joy may be in you and that your joy may be complete.

—**John 15:10–11**

I will extol the LORD at all times;
   his praise will always be on my lips.
My soul will boast in the LORD;
   let the afflicted hear and rejoice.
Glorify the LORD with me;
   let us exalt his name together.

I sought the LORD, and he answered me;
   he delivered me from all my fears.
Those who look to him are radiant;
   their faces are never covered with shame.

—**Psalm 34:1–5**

Tuesday

Be joyful always; pray continually; give thanks in all circumstances, for this is God's will for you in Christ Jesus.

—1 Thessalonians 5:16–18

Let the peace of Christ rule in your hearts, since as members of one body you were called to peace. And be thankful. Let the word of Christ dwell in you richly as you teach and admonish one another with all wisdom, and as you sing psalms, hymns and spiritual songs with gratitude in your hearts to God. And whatever you do, whether in word or deed, do it all in the name of the LORD Jesus, giving thanks to God the Father through him.

—Colossians 3:15–17

A fool finds pleasure in evil conduct,
    but a man of understanding delights
in wisdom.

—Proverbs 10:23

HAVING A GOOD ATTITUDE

Wednesday

An anxious heart weighs a man down,
  but a kind word cheers him up.

—**Proverbs 12:25**

A happy heart makes the face cheerful,
  but heartache crushes the spirit.

—**Proverbs 15:13**

All the days of the oppressed are wretched,
  but the cheerful heart has a continual feast.

—**Proverbs 15:15**

He will yet fill your mouth with laughter
and your lips with shouts of joy.

—**Job 8:21**

This is the day the LORD has made;
  let us rejoice and be glad in it.

—**Psalm 118:24**

HAVING A GOOD ATTITUDE

Thursday

So then, just as you received Christ Jesus as LORD, continue to live in him, rooted and built up in him, strengthened in the faith as you were taught, and overflowing with thankfulness.

—**Colossians 2:6–7**

I will rejoice in the LORD,
   I will be joyful in God my Savior.

The Sovereign LORD is my strength;
   he makes my feet like the feet of a deer,
   he enables me to go on the heights.

—**Habakkuk 3:18–19**

Let all who take refuge in you be glad;
   let them ever sing for joy.
Spread your protection over them,
   that those who love your name may rejoice
in you.

—**Psalm 5:11**

HAVING A GOOD ATTITUDE

Friday

Be patient, then, brothers, until the LORD's coming. See how the farmer waits for the land to yield its valuable crop and how patient he is for the autumn and spring rains. You too, be patient and stand firm, because the LORD's coming is near. Don't grumble against each other, brothers, or you will be judged. The Judge is standing at the door!

—James 5:7–9

Give thanks to the LORD, call on his name;
    make known among the nations what he
    has done.
Sing to him, sing praise to him;
    tell of all his wonderful acts.
Glory in his holy name;
    let the hearts of those who seek the
    LORD rejoice.

—1 Chronicles 16:8–10

HAVING A GOOD ATTITUDE

Weekend

NEHEMIAH SAID, "Go and enjoy choice food and sweet drinks, and send some to those who have nothing prepared. This day is sacred to our LORD. Do not grieve, for the joy of the LORD is your strength."

—**Nehemiah 8:10**

"**H**ear, O LORD, and be merciful to me;
O LORD, be my help."

You turned my wailing into dancing;
you removed my sackcloth and clothed me
with joy,
that my heart may sing to you and not be silent.
O LORD my God, I will give you
thanks forever.

—**Psalm 30:10–12**

Moreover, when God gives any man wealth and possessions, and enables him to enjoy them, to accept his lot and be happy in his work—this is a gift of God.

—**Ecclesiastes 5:19**

RESISTING TEMPTATION

Monday

My son, if sinners entice you,
  do not give in to them.
If they say, "Come along with us;
  let's lie in wait for someone's blood,
  let's waylay some harmless soul;
let's swallow them alive, like the grave,
  and whole, like those who go down to the pit;
we will get all sorts of valuable things
  and fill our houses with plunder;
throw in your lot with us,
  and we will share a common purse"—
my son, do not go along with them,
  do not set foot on their paths;
for their feet rush into sin,
  they are swift to shed blood.
How useless to spread a net
  in full view of all the birds!
These men lie in wait for their own blood;
    they waylay only themselves!
Such is the end of all who go after ill-gotten gain;
it takes away the lives of those who get it.

—**Proverbs 1:10–19**

Tuesday

Submit yourselves, then, to God. Resist the devil, and he will flee from you. Come near to God and he will come near to you.

—James 4:7–8

[**J**esus] shared in [our] humanity so that by his death he might destroy him who holds the power of death—that is, the devil— and free those who all their lives were held in slavery by their fear of death.

—Hebrews 2:14–15

For we do not have a high priest who is unable to sympathize with our weaknesses, but we have one who has been tempted in every way, just as we are—yet was without sin. Let us then approach the throne of grace with confidence, so that we may receive mercy and find grace to help us in our time of need.

—Hebrews 4:15–16

RESISTING TEMPTATION

Wednesday

When tempted, no one should say, "God is tempting me." For God cannot be tempted by evil, nor does he tempt anyone; but each one is tempted when, by his own evil desire, he is dragged away and enticed.

—James 1:13–14

Do not give the devil a foothold. He who has been stealing must steal no longer, but must work, doing something useful with his own hands, that he may have something to share with those in need.

—Ephesians 4:27–28

People who want to get rich fall into temptation and a trap and into many foolish and harmful desires that plunge men into ruin and destruction. For the love of money is a root of all kinds of evil. Some people, eager for money, have wandered from the faith and pierced themselves with many griefs.

—1 Timothy 6:9–10

Thursday

If we walk in the light, as he is in the light, we have fellowship with one another, and the blood of Jesus, his Son, purifies us from all sin. If we claim to be without sin, we deceive ourselves and the truth is not in us. If we confess our sins, he is faithful and just and will forgive us our sins and purify us from all unrighteousness.

—1 John 1:7–9

Your enemy the devil prowls around like a roaring lion looking for someone to devour. Resist him, standing firm in the faith, because you know that your brothers throughout the world are undergoing the same kind of sufferings.

—1 Peter 5:8–9

JESUS SAID TO HIS DISCIPLES:
"Watch and pray so that you will not fall into temptation. The spirit is willing, but the body is weak."

—Mark 14:38

Friday

Dear friend, do not imitate what is evil but what is good. Anyone who does what is good is from God. Anyone who does what is evil has not seen God.

—3 John 11

No temptation has seized you except what is common to man. And God is faithful; he will not let you be tempted beyond what you can bear. But when you are tempted, he will also provide a way out so that you can stand up under it. Therefore, my dear friends, flee from idolatry.

—1 Corinthians 10:13–14

Who can discern his errors?
  Forgive my hidden faults.
Keep your servant also from willful sins;
  may they not rule over me.
Then will I be blameless,
  innocent of great transgression.

—Psalm 19:12–13

RESISTING TEMPTATION

Weekend

Jesus was led by the Spirit into the desert to be tempted by the devil. After fasting forty days and forty nights, he was hungry. The tempter came to him and said, "If you are the Son of God, tell these stones to become bread."

Jesus answered, "It is written: 'Man does not live on bread alone, but on every word that comes from the mouth of God.' "

The devil took him to a very high mountain and showed him all the kingdoms of the world and their splendor. "All this I will give you," he said, "if you will bow down and worship me."

Jesus said to him, "Away from me, Satan! For it is written: 'Worship the LORD your God, and serve him only.' "

Then the devil left him.

—**Matthew 4:1–4, 8–11**

TALENTS AND GIFTS

Monday

"**A** man going on a journey ... called his servants and entrusted his property to them. To one he gave five talents of money, to another two talents, and to another one talent, each according to his ability. Then he went on his journey. The man who had received the five talents went at once and put his money to work and gained five more....

"After a long time the master of those servants returned and settled accounts with them. The man who had received the five talents brought the other five. 'Master,' he said, 'you entrusted me with five talents. See, I have gained five more.'

"His master replied, 'Well done, good and faithful servant! You have been faithful with a few things; I will put you in charge of many things. Come and share your master's happiness!'... For everyone who has will be given more, and he will have an abundance.

—**Matthew 25:14–16, 19–21, 29**

Tuesday

Sing joyfully to the LORD, you righteous;
  it is fitting for the upright to praise him.
Praise the LORD with the harp;
  make music to him on the ten-stringed lyre.
Sing to him a new song;
  play skillfully, and shout for joy.

—Psalm 33:1–3

My heart is steadfast, O God;
  I will sing and make music with all my soul.
Awake, harp and lyre!
  I will awaken the dawn.
I will praise you, O LORD, among the nations;
  I will sing of you among the peoples.
For great is your love, higher than the heavens;
  your faithfulness reaches to the skies.
Be exalted, O God, above the heavens,
  and let your glory be over all the earth.

—Psalm 108:1–5

Wednesday

We have different gifts, according to the grace given us. If a man's gift is prophesying, let him use it in proportion to his faith. If it is serving, let him serve; if it is teaching, let him teach; if it is encouraging, let him encourage; if it is contributing to the needs of others, let him give generously; if it is leadership, let him govern diligently; if it is showing mercy, let him do it cheerfully.

—Romans 12:6–8

For everything in heaven and earth is yours.
Yours, O LORD, is the kingdom;
  you are exalted as head over all.
Wealth and honor come from you...
In your hands are strength and power
  to exalt and give strength to all.

—1 Chronicles 29:11–12

Thursday

Each man has his own gift from God; one has this gift, another has that.

— **1 Corinthians 7:7**

Each one should use whatever gift he has received to serve others, faithfully administering God's grace in its various forms.

— **1 Peter 4:10**

Moses said to the LORD, "O LORD, I have never been eloquent, neither in the past nor since you have spoken to your servant. I am slow of speech and tongue."

The LORD said to him, "Who gave man his mouth? Who makes him deaf or mute? Who gives him sight or makes him blind? Is it not I, the LORD? Now go; I will help you speak and will teach you what to say."

— **Exodus 4:10–12**

TALENTS AND GIFTS

Friday

Every good and perfect gift is from above, coming down from the Father of the heavenly lights, who does not change like shifting shadows.

—James 1:17

Then Moses summoned Bezalel and Oholiab and every skilled person to whom the LORD had given ability and who was willing to come and do the work.

—Exodus 36:2

Adah gave birth to Jabal; he was the father of those who live in tents and raise livestock. His brother's name was Jubal; he was the father of all who play the harp and flute. Zillah also had a son, Tubal-Cain, who forged all kinds of tools out of bronze and iron.

—Genesis 4:20–22

"**F**or the entrance to the tent make a curtain of blue, purple and scarlet yarn and finely twisted linen—the work of an embroiderer."

—Exodus 26:36

TALENTS AND GIFTS

Weekend

You may say to yourself, "My power and the strength of my hands have produced this wealth for me." But remember the LORD your God, for it is he who gives you the ability to produce wealth, and so confirms his covenant, which he swore to your forefathers, as it is today.

—**Deuteronomy 8:17–18**

Now, our God, we give you thanks,
and praise your glorious name.

"But who am I, and who are my people, that we should be able to give as generously as this? Everything comes from you, and we have given you only what comes from your hand."

—**1 Chronicles 29:13–14**

By the grace given me I say to every one of you: Do not think of yourself more highly than you ought, but rather think of yourself with sober judgment, in accordance with the measure of faith God has given you.

—**Romans 12:3**

THE IMPORTANCE OF HARD WORK

Monday

Make it your ambition to lead a quiet life, to mind your own business and to work with your hands, just as we told you, so that your daily life may win the respect of outsiders and so that you will not be dependent on anybody.

—**1 Thessalonians 4:11–12**

Whatever you do, work at it with all your heart, as working for the LORD, not for men, since you know that you will receive an inheritance from the LORD as a reward. It is the LORD Christ you are serving.

—**Colossians 3:23–24**

The way of the sluggard is blocked with thorns, but the path of the upright is a highway.

—**Proverbs 15:19**

It is good and proper for a man to eat and drink, and to find satisfaction in his toilsome labor under the sun during the few days of life God has given him—for this is his lot.

—**Ecclesiastes 5:18**

Tuesday

The sluggard buries his hand in the dish;
   he will not even bring it back to his mouth!

—**Proverbs 19:24**

"As for you, be strong and do not give up, for
your work will be rewarded."

—**2 Chronicles 15:7**

NEHEMIAH SAID:
[Those who opposed our project] were all trying
to frighten us, thinking, "Their hands will get too
weak for the work, and it will not be completed."
But I prayed, "Now strengthen my hands."

—**Nehemiah 6:9**

"The Israelites had done all the work just as the
LORD had commanded Moses. Moses inspected
the work and saw that they had done it just
as the LORD had commanded. So Moses
blessed them.

—**Exodus 39:42–44**

Wednesday

Do you not know that in a race all the runners run, but only one gets the prize? Run in such a way as to get the prize.

—1 Corinthians 9:24

May the favor of the LORD our God rest upon us;
establish the work of our hands for us—
yes, establish the work of our hands.

—Psalm 90:17

My heart took delight in all my work,
and this was the reward for all my labor.

—Ecclesiastes 2:10

All hard work brings a profit,
but mere talk leads only to poverty.

—Proverbs 14:23

Thursday

Do not love sleep or you will grow poor;
    stay awake and you will have food to spare.

—**Proverbs 20:13**

Do you see a man skilled in his work?
    He will serve before kings;
    he will not serve before obscure men.

—**Proverbs 22:29**

Do your best to present yourself to God as one
approved, a workman who does not need to be
ashamed and who correctly handles the word
of truth.

—**2 Timothy 2:15**

He who works his land will have abundant food,
    but he who chases fantasies lacks judgment.

—**Proverbs 12:11**

Friday

A sluggard does not plow in season;
so at harvest time he looks but finds nothing.

—Proverbs 20:4

To this end I labor, struggling with all his
energy, which so powerfully works in me.

—Colossians 1:29

He who gathers crops in summer is a wise son,
but he who sleeps during harvest is a disgrace-
ful son.

—Proverbs 10:5

David also said to Solomon his son, "Be strong
and courageous, and do the work. Do not be
afraid or discouraged, for the LORD God, my
God, is with you. He will not fail you or forsake
you until all the work for the service of the temple of the LORD is finished."

—1 Chronicles 28:20

THE IMPORTANCE OF HARD WORK

Weekend

The plans of the diligent lead to profit
   as surely as haste leads to poverty.

—**Proverbs 21:5**

He who loves pleasure will become poor;
   whoever loves wine and oil will never be rich.

—**Proverbs 21:17**

Go to the ant, you sluggard;
   consider its ways and be wise!
It has no commander,
   no overseer or ruler,
yet it stores its provisions in summer
   and gathers its food at harvest.

How long will you lie there, you sluggard?
   When will you get up from your sleep?
A little sleep, a little slumber,
   a little folding of the hands to rest—
and poverty will come on you like a bandit
   and scarcity like an armed man.

—**Proverbs 6:6–11**

MAKING CHOICES

Monday

Stop doing wrong,
  learn to do right!
Seek justice,
  encourage the oppressed.
Defend the cause of the fatherless,
  plead the case of the widow.
"Come now, let us reason together,"
  says the LORD.
"Though your sins are like scarlet,
  they shall be as white as snow;
though they are red as crimson,
  they shall be like wool.
If you are willing and obedient,
  you will eat the best from the land;
but if you resist and rebel,
  you will be devoured by the sword."
For the mouth of the LORD has spoken.

—Isaiah 1:16–20

MAKING CHOICES

Tuesday

"**F**ear the LORD and serve him with all faithfulness. Throw away the gods your forefathers worshiped beyond the River and in Egypt, and serve the LORD. But if serving the LORD seems undesirable to you, then choose for yourselves this day whom you will serve, whether the gods your forefathers served beyond the River, or the gods of the Amorites, in whose land you are living. But as for me and my household, we will serve the LORD."

—Joshua 24:14–15

Blessed are they who maintain justice,
who constantly do what is right.

—Psalm 106:3

How much better to get wisdom than gold,
to choose understanding rather than silver!

—Proverbs 16:16

MAKING CHOICES

Wednesday

This day I call heaven and earth as witnesses against you that I have set before you life and death, blessings and curses. Now choose life, so that you and your children may live and that you may love the LORD your God, listen to his voice, and hold fast to him. For the LORD is your life, and he will give you many years in the land he swore to give to your fathers, Abraham, Isaac and Jacob.

—Deuteronomy 30:19–20

Be very careful, then, how you live—not as unwise but as wise, making the most of every opportunity, because the days are evil.

—Ephesians 5:15–16

Fear God and keep his commandments,
  for this is the whole duty of man.
For God will bring every deed into judgment,
  including every hidden thing,
  whether it is good or evil.

—Ecclesiastes 12:13–14

WEEK 7

MAKING CHOICES

Thursday

Blessed is the man
   who does not walk in the counsel of
the wicked
    or stand in the way of sinners
    or sit in the seat of mockers.
But his delight is in the law of the LORD,
   and on his law he meditates day and night.

—Psalm 1:1–2

"**S**ince they hated knowledge
   and did not choose to fear the LORD,
since they would not accept my advice
   and spurned my rebuke,
they will eat the fruit of their ways
   and be filled with the fruit of their schemes.
For the waywardness of the simple will kill them,
   and the complacency of fools will
destroy them;
but whoever listens to me will live in safety
   and be at ease, without fear of harm."

—Proverbs 1:29–33

MAKING CHOICES

Friday

Remember how the LORD your God led you all the way in the desert these forty years, to humble you and to test you in order to know what was in your heart, whether or not you would keep his commands.

—Deuteronomy 8:2

"**S**tand at the crossroads and look;
    ask for the ancient paths,
ask where the good way is, and walk in it,
    and you will find rest for your souls."

—Jeremiah 6:16

Remember your Creator
    in the days of your youth.

—Ecclesiastes 12:1

Weekend

The LORD your God is testing you to find out whether you love him with all your heart and with all your soul. It is the LORD your God you must follow, and him you must revere. Keep his commands and obey him; serve him and hold fast to him.

—Deuteronomy 13:3–4

He who has suffered in his body is done with sin. As a result, he does not live the rest of his earthly life for evil human desires, but rather for the will of God. For you have spent enough time in the past doing what pagans choose to do.... They think it strange that you do not plunge with them into the same flood of dissipation, and they heap abuse on you. But they will have to give account to him who is ready to judge the living and the dead. The gospel was preached ... so that they might be judged according to men in regard to the body, but live according to God in regard to the spirit. The end of all things is near. Therefore be clear minded and self-controlled so that you can pray.

—1 Peter 4:1–7

ACCEPTING THE CONSEQUENCES
OF OUR CHOICES

Monday

The LORD has dealt with me according to
my righteousness;
  according to the cleanness of my hands he
has rewarded me.
For I have kept the ways of the LORD;
  I have not done evil by turning from my God.
All his laws are before me;
  I have not turned away from his decrees.
I have been blameless before him
  and have kept myself from sin.
The LORD has rewarded me according to
my righteousness,
  according to the cleanness of my hands in
his sight.

To the faithful you show yourself faithful,
  to the blameless you show yourself blameless,
to the pure you show yourself pure,
  but to the crooked you show yourself shrewd.

—Psalm 18:20–26

Tuesday

Do not be deceived: God cannot be mocked. A man reaps what he sows. The one who sows to please his sinful nature, from that nature will reap destruction; the one who sows to please the Spirit will reap eternal life.

—**Galatians 6:7–8**

Anyone who does wrong will be repaid for his wrong, and there is no favoritism.

—**Colossians 3:25**

One thing God has spoken,
   two things have I heard:
that you, O God, are strong,
   and that you, O LORD, are loving.
Surely you will reward each person
   according to what he has done.

—**Psalm 62:11–12**

ACCEPTING THE CONSEQUENCES OF OUR CHOICES

Wednesday

"Make a tree good and its fruit will be good, or make a tree bad and its fruit will be bad, for a tree is recognized by its fruit. You brood of vipers, how can you who are evil say anything good? For out of the overflow of the heart the mouth speaks. The good man brings good things out of the good stored up in him, and the evil man brings evil things out of the evil stored up in him. But I tell you that men will have to give account on the day of judgment for every careless word they have spoken. For by your words you will be acquitted, and by your words you will be condemned."

—Matthew 12:33–37

Can both fresh water and salt water flow from the same spring? My brothers, can a fig tree bear olives, or a grapevine bear figs? Neither can a salt spring produce fresh water.

—James 3:11–12

Thursday

Land that drinks in the rain often falling on it and that produces a crop useful to those for whom it is farmed receives the blessing of God. But land that produces thorns and thistles is worthless and is in danger of being cursed. In the end it will be burned.

Even though we speak like this, dear friends, we are confident of better things in your case—things that accompany salvation. God is not unjust; he will not forget your work and the love you have shown him as you have helped his people and continue to help them.

—Hebrews 6:7–10

"Behold, I am coming soon! My reward is with me, and I will give to everyone according to what he has done. I am the Alpha and the Omega, the First and the Last, the Beginning and the End."

—Revelation 22:12–13

Friday

Remember this: Whoever sows sparingly will also reap sparingly, and whoever sows generously will also reap generously. Each man should give what he has decided in his heart to give, not reluctantly or under compulsion, for God loves a cheerful giver. And God is able to make all grace abound to you, so that in all things at all times, having all that you need, you will abound in every good work. As it is written: "He has scattered abroad his gifts to the poor; his righteousness endures forever."

Now he who supplies seed to the sower and bread for food will also supply and increase your store of seed and will enlarge the harvest of your righteousness. You will be made rich in every way so that you can be generous on every occasion, and through us your generosity will result in thanksgiving to God.

—**2 Corinthians 9:6–11**

ACCEPTING THE CONSEQUENCES OF OUR CHOICES

Weekend

He who works his land will have abundant food,
   but the one who chases fantasies will have
his fill of poverty.

—**Proverbs 28:19**

The sins of some men are obvious, reaching the
place of judgment ahead of them; the sins of others trail behind them. In the same way, good
deeds are obvious, and even those that are not
cannot be hidden.

—**1 Timothy 5:24–25**

What the wicked dreads will overtake him;
   what the righteous desire will be granted.

—**Proverbs 10:24**

The wages of the righteous bring them life,
   but the income of the wicked brings them
punishment.

—**Proverbs10:16**

AVOIDING BAD HABITS

Monday

Who has woe? Who has sorrow?
  Who has strife? Who has complaints?
  Who has needless bruises? Who has blood-
shot eyes?
Those who linger over wine,
  who go to sample bowls of mixed wine.
Do not gaze at wine when it is red,
  when it sparkles in the cup,
  when it goes down smoothly!
In the end it bites like a snake
  and poisons like a viper.
Your eyes will see strange sights
  and your mind imagine confusing things.
You will be like one sleeping on the high seas,
  lying on top of the rigging.
"They hit me," you will say, "but I'm not hurt!
  They beat me, but I don't feel it!
When will I wake up
  so I can find another drink?"

—**Proverbs 23:29–35**

Tuesday

Put to death, therefore, whatever belongs to your earthly nature: sexual immorality, impurity, lust, evil desires and greed, which is idolatry. Because of these, the wrath of God is coming. You used to walk in these ways, in the life you once lived. But now you must rid yourselves of all such things as these: anger, rage, malice, slander, and filthy language from your lips. Do not lie to each other, since you have taken off your old self with its practices and have put on the new self, which is being renewed in knowledge in the image of its Creator. Here there is no Greek or Jew, circumcised or uncircumcised, barbarian, Scythian, slave or free, but Christ is all, and is in all.

Therefore, as God's chosen people, holy and dearly loved, clothe yourselves with compassion, kindness, humility, gentleness and patience. Bear with each other and forgive whatever grievances you may have against one another. Forgive as the LORD forgave you. And over all these virtues put on love, which binds them all together in perfect unity.

—Colossians 3:5–14

Wednesday

But among you there must not be even a hint of sexual immorality, or of any kind of impurity, or of greed, because these are improper for God's holy people. Nor should there be obscenity, foolish talk or coarse joking, ... but rather thanksgiving.... No immoral, impure or greedy person ... has any inheritance in the kingdom of Christ and of God. Let no one deceive you with empty words, for because of such things God's wrath comes on those who are disobedient. Therefore do not be partners with them.

—Ephesians 5:3–7

If you make the Most High your dwelling-
   even the LORD, who is my refugethen
no harm will befall you,
   no disaster will come near your tent.
For he will command his angels concerning you
   to guard you in all your ways;
they will lift you up in their hands,
   so that you will not strike your foot against
a stone.

—Psalm 91:9–12

Thursday

Above all, my brothers, do not swear—not by heaven or by earth or by anything else. Let your "Yes" be yes, and your "No," no, or you will be condemned.

—**James 5:12**

Whoever of you loves life
  and desires to see many good days,
keep your tongue from evil
  and your lips from speaking lies.
Turn from evil and do good;
  seek peace and pursue it.

—**Psalm 34:11–14**

Likewise the tongue is a small part of the body, but it makes great boasts. Consider what a great forest is set on fire by a small spark. The tongue also is a fire, a world of evil among the parts of the body. It corrupts the whole person, sets the whole course of his life on fire, and is itself set on fire by hell.

—**James 3:5–6**

Friday

For the grace of God that brings salvation has appeared to all men. It teaches us to say "No" to ungodliness and worldly passions, and to live self-controlled, upright and godly lives in this present age, while we wait for the blessed hope—the glorious appearing of our great God and Savior, Jesus Christ.

—Titus 2:11–13

The hour has come for you to wake up from your slumber, because our salvation is nearer now than when we first believed. The night is nearly over; the day is almost here. So let us put aside the deeds of darkness and put on the armor of light. Let us behave decently, as in the daytime, not in orgies and drunkenness, not in sexual immorality and debauchery, not in dissension and jealousy. Rather, clothe yourselves with the LORD Jesus Christ, and do not think about how to gratify the desires of the sinful nature.

—Romans 13:11–14

Weekend

The wrath of God is being revealed from heaven against all the godlessness and wickedness of men who suppress the truth by their wickedness, ...

For although they knew God, they neither glorified him as God nor gave thanks to him, but their thinking became futile and their foolish hearts were darkened....

"Because of this, God gave them over to shameful lusts. Even their women exchanged natural relations for unnatural ones.... Men committed indecent acts with other men, and received in themselves the due penalty for their perversion. Furthermore, since they did not think it worthwhile to retain the knowledge of God, he gave them over to a depraved mind, to do what ought not to be done. They have become filled with every kind of wickedness.... Although they know God's righteous decree that those who do such things deserve death, they not only continue to do these very things but also approve of those who practice them.

—**Romans 1:18, 21, 26–29, 32**

BECOMING WISE

Monday

Hold on to instruction, do not let it go;
  guard it well, for it is your life.
Do not set foot on the path of the wicked
  or walk in the way of evil men.
Avoid it, do not travel on it;
  turn from it and go on your way.
For they cannot sleep till they do evil;
  they are robbed of slumber till they make
someone fall.
They eat the bread of wickedness
  and drink the wine of violence.

The path of the righteous is like the first gleam
of dawn,
  shining ever brighter till the full light of day.
But the way of the wicked is like deep darkness;
  they do not know what makes them stumble.

—**Proverbs 4:13–19**

Tuesday

"**W**here then does wisdom come from?
     Where does understanding dwell?
It is hidden from the eyes of every living thing,
     concealed even from the birds of the air.
Destruction and Death say,
     'Only a rumor of it has reached our ears.'
God understands the way to it
     and he alone knows where it dwells,
for he views the ends of the earth
     and sees everything under the heavens.
When he established the force of the wind
     and measured out the waters,
when he made a decree for the rain
     and a path for the thunderstorm,
then he looked at wisdom and appraised it;
     he confirmed it and tested it.
And he said to man,
     'The fear of the LORD—that is wisdom,
     and to shun evil is understanding.' "

—Job 28:20–28

Wednesday

If any of you lacks wisdom, he should ask God, who gives generously to all without finding fault, and it will be given to him. But when he asks, he must believe and not doubt, because he who doubts is like a wave of the sea, blown and tossed by the wind.

—James 1:5–6

"Where is the wise man? Where is the scholar? Where is the philosopher of this age? ... the world through its wisdom did not know him, God was pleased through the foolishness of what was preached to save those who believe. Jews demand miraculous signs and Greeks look for wisdom, but we preach Christ crucified: a stumbling block to Jews and foolishness to Gentiles, but to those whom God has called, both Jews and Greeks, Christ the power of God and the wisdom of God. For the foolishness of God is wiser than man's wisdom, and the weakness of God is stronger than man's strength.

—1 Corinthians 1:20–25

Thursday

Do not deceive yourselves. If any one of you thinks he is wise by the standards of this age, he should become a "fool" so that he may become wise. For the wisdom of this world is foolishness in God's sight. As it is written: "He catches the wise in their craftiness"; and again, "The LORD knows that the thoughts of the wise are futile." So then, no more boasting about men! All things are yours, ... and you are of Christ, and Christ is of God.

—1 Corinthians 3:18–21, 23

WISDOM SAYS:
"Counsel and sound judgment are mine;
  I have understanding and power.
By me kings reign
  and rulers make laws that are just;
by me princes govern,
  and all nobles who rule on earth.
I love those who love me,
  and those who seek me find me."

—Proverbs 8:14–17

Friday

When a farmer plows for planting, does he
plow continually?
  Does he keep on breaking up and harrowing
the soil?
When he has leveled the surface,
  does he not sow caraway and scatter cummin?
Does he not plant wheat in its place,
  barley in its plot,
  and spelt in its field?
His God instructs him
  and teaches him the right way.

Caraway is not threshed with a sledge,
  nor is a cartwheel rolled over cummin;
caraway is beaten out with a rod,
  and cummin with a stick.
Grain must be ground to make bread;
  so one does not go on threshing it forever....
All this also comes from the LORD Almighty,
  wonderful in counsel and magnificent
in wisdom.

—Isaiah 28:24–29

Weekend

The holy Scriptures ... are able to make you wise for salvation through faith in Christ Jesus. All Scripture is God-breathed and is useful for teaching, rebuking, correcting and training in righteousness, so that the man of God may be thoroughly equipped for every good work.

—**2 Timothy 3:15–17**

The word of God ... [divides] soul and spirit, joints and marrow; it judges the thoughts and attitudes of the heart.

—**Hebrews 4:12**

Oh, how I love your law!
I meditate on it all day long.
Your commands make me wiser than
my enemies,
for they are ever with me.
I have more insight than all my teachers,
for I meditate on your statutes.
I have more understanding than the elders,
for I obey your precepts.

—**Psalm 119:97–100**

BEING DISCERNING

Monday

The fool says in his heart,
  "There is no God."
They are corrupt, their deeds are vile;
  there is no one who does good.

The LORD looks down from heaven
  on the sons of men
to see if there are any who understand,
  any who seek God.
All have turned aside,
  they have together become corrupt;
there is no one who does good,
  not even one.

—Psalm 14:1–3

The wise in heart are called discerning,
  and pleasant words promote instruction.

—Proverbs 16:21

Tuesday

Be as shrewd as snakes and as innocent as doves. Be on your guard.

—**Matthew 10:16–17**

Who is wise? He will realize these things.
Who is discerning? He will understand them.
The ways of the LORD are right;
the righteous walk in them,
but the rebellious stumble in them.

—**Hosea 14:9**

The mocker seeks wisdom and finds none,
but knowledge comes easily to the discerning.

—**Proverbs 14:6**

My son, preserve sound judgment
and discernment,
do not let them out of your sight.

—**Proverbs 3:21**

Wednesday

Wisdom is found on the lips of the discerning,
   but a rod is for the back of him who
lacks judgment.

—**Proverbs 10:13**

Test everything. Hold on to the good. Avoid
every kind of evil. May God himself, the God of
peace, sanctify you through and through. May
your whole spirit, soul and body be kept blameless at the coming of our LORD Jesus Christ. The
one who calls you is faithful and he will do it.

—**1 Thessalonians 5:21–24**

For the ear tests words
   as the tongue tastes food.
Let us discern for ourselves what is right;
   let us learn together what is good.

—**Job 34:3–4**

Thursday

At *Gibeon the* LORD *appeared to Solomon during the night in a dream, and God said, "Ask for whatever you want me to give you."*

Solomon answered, "You have shown great kindness to your servant, my father David. ... You have continued this great kindness to him and have given him a son to sit on his throne this very day. "Now, O LORD my God, you have made your servant king in place of my father David. But I am only a little child and do not know how to carry out my duties.... So give your servant a discerning heart to govern your people and to distinguish between right and wrong."

The LORD was pleased [with this]. "I will do what you have asked. I will give you a wise and discerning heart.... Moreover, I will give you what you have not asked for—both riches and honor—so that in your lifetime you will have no equal among kings. And if you walk in my ways and obey my statutes and commands as David your father did, I will give you a long life."

—1 Kings 3:5–7, 9–10, 12–14

Friday

A rebuke impresses a man of discernment
more than a hundred lashes a fool.

—**Proverbs 17:10**

The discerning heart seeks knowledge,
but the mouth of a fool feeds on folly.

—**Proverbs 15:14**

JESUS SAID:
"*Wisdom is proved right by her actions.*"

—**Matthew 11:19**

A simple man believes anything,
but a prudent man gives thought to his steps.

—**Proverbs 14:15**

Weekend

A prudent man sees danger and takes refuge,
  but the simple keep going and suffer for it.

—**Proverbs 22:3**

[**T**he LORD] guards the course of the just
  and protects the way of his faithful ones.
Then you will understand what is right and just
  and fair—every good path.
For wisdom will enter your heart,
  and knowledge will be pleasant to your soul.
Discretion will protect you,
  and understanding will guard you.

—**Proverbs 2:8–11**

Wisdom reposes in the heart of the discerning.

—**Proverbs 14:33**

CHOOSING GOOD FRIENDS

Monday

A friend loves at all times,
and a brother is born for adversity.

—**Proverbs 17:17**

Two are better than one,
   because they have a good return for
their work:
If one falls down,
   his friend can help him up.
But pity the man who falls
   and has no one to help him up!
Also, if two lie down together, they will
keep warm.
   But how can one keep warm alone?
Though one may be overpowered,
   two can defend themselves.
A cord of three strands is not quickly broken.

—**Ecclesiastes 4:9–12**

The LORD would speak to Moses face to face,
   as a man speaks with his friend.

—**Exodus 33:11**

CHOOSING GOOD FRIENDS

Tuesday

Listen to my prayer, O God,
  do not ignore my plea;
  hear me and answer me.
My thoughts trouble me and I
am distraught...
If an enemy were insulting me,
  I could endure it;
if a foe were raising himself against me,
  I could hide from him.
But it is you, a man like myself,
  my companion, my close friend,
with whom I once enjoyed sweet fellowship
  as we walked with the throng at the house
of God.

—Psalm 55:1–2, 12–14

Even my close friend, whom I trusted,
  he who shared my bread,
  has lifted up his heel against me.

—Psalm 41:9

CHOOSING GOOD FRIENDS

Wednesday

He who walks with the wise grows wise,
  but a companion of fools suffers harm.

—Proverbs 13:20

Do not be misled: "Bad company corrupts
good character."

—1 Corinthians 15:33

He who keeps the law is a discerning son,
  but a companion of gluttons disgraces
his father.

—Proverbs 28:7

I am a friend to all who fear you,
  to all who follow your precepts.

—Psalm 119:63

CHOOSING GOOD FRIENDS

Thursday

Do not make friends with a hot-tempered man,
   do not associate with one easily angered,
or you may learn his ways
   and get yourself ensnared.

—Proverbs 22:24–25

A man of many companions may come to ruin,
   but there is a friend who sticks closer than
a brother.

—Proverbs 18:24

The LORD does not look at the things man looks
at. Man looks at the outward appearance, but
the LORD looks at the heart.

—1 Samuel 16:7

Stay away from a foolish man,
for you will not find knowledge on his lips.

—Proverbs 14:7

CHOOSING GOOD FRIENDS

Friday

Listen, my son, and be wise,
and keep your heart on the right path.
Do not join those who drink too much wine
or gorge themselves on meat,
for drunkards and gluttons become poor,
and drowsiness clothes them in rags.

—Proverbs 23:19–21

Anyone who chooses to be a friend of the world
becomes an enemy of God.

—James 4:4

A righteous man is cautious in friendship,
but the way of the wicked leads them astray.

—Proverbs 12:26

CHOOSING GOOD FRIENDS

Weekend

Do not envy wicked men,
    do not desire their company;
for their hearts plot violence,
    and their lips talk about making trouble.

—**Proverbs 24:1–2**

A man who loves wisdom brings joy to
his father,
    but a companion of prostitutes squanders
his wealth.

—**Proverbs 29:3**

As for those who seemed to be important—
whatever they were makes no difference to me;
God does not judge by external appearance.

—**Galatians 2:6**

ANTIDOTE FOR WORRY

Monday

Cast your cares on the LORD
and he will sustain you;
he will never let the righteous fall.

—Psalm 55:22

JESUS SAID:
"Do not let your hearts be troubled. Trust in
God; trust also in me."

—John 14:1

If the LORD delights in a man's way,
   he makes his steps firm;
though he stumble, he will not fall,
   for the LORD upholds him with his hand.

I was young and now I am old,
   yet I have never seen the righteous forsaken
   or their children begging bread.
They are always generous and lend freely;
   their children will be blessed.

—Psalm 37:23–26

ANTIDOTE FOR WORRY

Tuesday

Have no fear of sudden disaster
 or of the ruin that overtakes the wicked,
for the LORD will be your confidence
 and will keep your foot from being snared.

—**Proverbs 3:25–26**

"Because he loves me," says the LORD, "I will
 rescue him;
 I will protect him, for he acknowledges my
 name.
He will call upon me, and I will answer him;
 I will be with him in trouble,
 I will deliver him and honor him.
With long life will I satisfy him
 and show him my salvation."

—**Psalm 91:14–16**

The LORD gives strength to his people;
 the LORD blesses his people with peace.

—**Psalm 29:11**

ANTIDOTE FOR WORRY

Wednesday

The LORD is gracious and compassionate,
  slow to anger and rich in love.
The LORD is good to all;
  he has compassion on all he has made.
All you have made will praise you, O LORD;
  your saints will extol you.
They will tell of the glory of your kingdom
  and speak of your might,
so that all men may know of your mighty acts
  and the glorious splendor of your kingdom....
The LORD is faithful to all his promises
  and loving toward all he has made.
The LORD upholds all those who fall
  and lifts up all who are bowed down.
The eyes of all look to you,
  and you give them their food at the
proper time.
You open your hand
  and satisfy the desires of every living thing.

—Psalm 145:8–16

Thursday

"Though the mountains be shaken
   and the hills be removed,
yet my unfailing love for you will not be shaken
   nor my covenant of peace be removed,"
   says the LORD, who has compassion on you.

—**Isaiah 54:10**

"But blessed is the man who trusts in the LORD,
   whose confidence is in him.
He will be like a tree planted by the water
   that sends out its roots by the stream.
It does not fear when heat comes;
   its leaves are always green.
It has no worries in a year of drought
   and never fails to bear fruit."

—**Jeremiah 17:7–8**

Friday

Jesus said to his disciples: "Therefore I tell you, do not worry about your life, what you will eat; or about your body, what you will wear. Life is more than food, and the body more than clothes. Consider the ravens: They do not sow or reap, they have no storeroom or barn; yet God feeds them. And how much more valuable you are than birds! Who of you by worrying can add a single hour to his life? Since you cannot do this very little thing, why do you worry about the rest? "Consider how the lilies grow. They do not labor or spin. Yet I tell you, not even Solomon in all his splendor was dressed like one of these. If that is how God clothes the grass of the field, which is here today, and tomorrow is thrown into the fire, how much more will he clothe you, O you of little faith! And do not set your heart on what you will eat or drink; do not worry about it. For the pagan world runs after all such things, and your Father knows that you need them. But seek his kingdom, and these things will be given to you as well.

—Luke 12:22–31

Weekend

God is our refuge and strength,
  an ever-present help in trouble.
Therefore we will not fear, though the earth
give way
  and the mountains fall into the heart of the sea,
though its waters roar and foam
  and the mountains quake with their surging....
Come and see the works of the LORD,
  the desolations he has brought on the earth.
He makes wars cease to the ends of the earth;
  he breaks the bow and shatters the spear,
  he burns the shields with fire.
"Be still, and know that I am God;
  I will be exalted among the nations,
  I will be exalted in the earth."
The LORD Almighty is with us;
  the God of Jacob is our fortress.

—Psalm 46:1–3, 8–11

Monday

Let us fix our eyes on Jesus, the author and per-fecter of our faith, who for the joy set before him endured the cross, scorning its shame, and sat down at the right hand of the throne of God. Consider him who endured such opposition from sinful men, so that you will not grow weary and lose heart.

—**Hebrews 12:2–3**

JESUS SAID:
"I am the vine; you are the branches. If a man remains in me and I in him, he will bear much fruit; apart from me you can do nothing. If any-one does not remain in me, he is like a branch that is thrown away and withers; such branches are picked up, thrown into the fire and burned. If you remain in me and my words remain in you, ask whatever you wish, and it will be given you. This is to my Father's glory, that you bear much fruit, showing yourselves to *be my disciples.*"

—**John 15:5–8**

Tuesday

Since, then, you have been raised with Christ, set your hearts on things above, where Christ is seated at the right hand of God. Set your minds on things above, not on earthly things.

—**Colossians 3:1–2**

Whatever is true, whatever is noble, whatever is right, whatever is pure, whatever is lovely, whatever is admirable—if anything is excellent or praiseworthy—think about such things.

—**Philippians 4:8**

My eyes are fixed on you, O Sovereign LORD;
in you I take refuge—do not give me over to death.

—**Psalm 141:8**

A CLEAR FOCUS

Wednesday

I know my transgressions,
   and my sin is always before me.
Against you, you only, have I sinned
   and done what is evil in your sight,
so that you are proved right when you speak
   and justified when you judge.
Surely I was sinful at birth,
   sinful from the time my mother conceived me.
Surely you desire truth in the inner parts;
   you teach me wisdom in the inmost place.

—Psalm 51:3–6

A discerning man keeps wisdom in view,
   but a fool's eyes wander to the ends of
the earth.

—Proverbs 17:24

Thursday

Let your eyes look straight ahead,
  fix your gaze directly before you.
*Make level paths for your feet
  and take only ways that are firm.*
Do not swerve to the right or the left;
  keep your foot from evil.

—**Proverbs 4:25–27**

Great peace have they who love your law,
  and nothing can make them stumble.

—**Psalm 119:165**

The worries of this life and the deceitfulness of wealth choke [the message of the kingdom], making it unfruitful.

—**Matthew 13:22**

A CLEAR FOCUS

Friday

As for man, his days are like grass,
  he flourishes like a flower of the field;
the wind blows over it and it is gone,
  and its place remembers it no more.
But from everlasting to everlasting
  the LORD's love is with those who fear him,
  and his righteousness with their
children's children—
with those who keep his covenant
  and remember to obey his precepts.

—Psalm 103:15–18

PAUL WRITES:

I press on to take hold of that for which Christ
Jesus took hold of me. Brothers, I do not consider
myself yet to have taken hold of it. But one thing
I do: Forgetting what is behind and straining
toward what is ahead, I press on toward the goal
to win the prize for which God has called me
heavenward in Christ Jesus.

—Philippians 3:12–14

WEEK 14

A CLEAR FOCUS

Weekend

You will keep in perfect peace
  him whose mind is steadfast,
  because he trusts in you.
Trust in the LORD forever,
  for the LORD, the LORD, is the Rock eternal.

—Isaiah 26:3–4

As Jesus and his disciples were on their way, he came to a village where a woman named Martha opened her home to him. She had a sister called Mary, who sat at the LORD's feet listening to what he said. But Martha was distracted by all the preparations that had to be made. She came to him and asked, "LORD, don't you care that my sister has left me to do the work by myself? Tell her to help me!"

" Martha, Martha," the LORD answered, "you are worried and upset about many things, but only one thing is needed. Mary has chosen what is better, and it will not be taken away from her."

—Luke 10:38–42

Monday

Therefore each of you must put off falsehood and speak truthfully to his neighbor, for we are all members of one body.

—Ephesians 4:25

You destroy those who tell lies;
    bloodthirsty and deceitful men
    the LORD abhors.

—Psalm 5:6

A fortune made by a lying tongue
    is a fleeting vapor and a deadly snare.

—Proverbs 21:6

I will maintain my righteousness and never let go of it;
    my conscience will not reproach me as long as I live.

—Job 27:6

Tuesday

Therefore, rid yourselves of all malice and all deceit, hypocrisy, envy, and slander of every kind.

—1 Peter 2:1

God is not a man, that he should lie,
    nor a son of man, that he should change
his mind.
Does he speak and then not act?
    Does he promise and not fulfill?

—Numbers 23:19

The heart is deceitful above all things
    and beyond cure.
    Who can understand it?

"I the LORD search the heart
and examine the mind,
to reward a man according to his conduct,
according to what his deeds deserve."

—Jeremiah 17:9–10

Wednesday

An honest answer
    is like a kiss on the lips.

—**Proverbs 24:26**

"Go up and down the streets of Jerusalem,
    look around and consider,
    search through her squares.
If you can find but one person
    who deals honestly and seeks the truth,
    I will forgive this city.
Although they say, 'As surely as the LORD lives,'
    still they are swearing falsely."

O LORD, do not your eyes look for truth?

—**Jeremiah 5:1–3**

Like a madman shooting
    firebrands or deadly arrows
is a man who deceives his neighbor
    and says, "I was only joking!"

—**Proverbs 26:18–19**

BEING HONEST

Thursday

Why do you boast of evil, you mighty man?
  Why do you boast all day long,
  you who are a disgrace in the eyes of God?
Your tongue plots destruction;
  it is like a sharpened razor,
  you who practice deceit.
You love evil rather than good,
  falsehood rather than speaking the truth.
You love every harmful word,
  O you deceitful tongue!

Surely God will bring you down to
everlasting ruin:
  He will snatch you up and tear you from
your tent;
  he will uproot you from the land of the living.

—**Psalm 52:1–5**

Friday

I *will walk in my house*
with blameless heart.
I will set before my eyes
no vile thing.

The deeds of faithless men I hate;
they will not cling to me.
Men of perverse heart shall be far from me;
I will have nothing to do with evil.

Whoever slanders his neighbor in secret,
him will I put to silence;
whoever has haughty eyes and a proud heart,
him will I not endure.

My eyes will be on the faithful in the land,
that they may dwell with me;
he whose walk is blameless
will minister to me.

—Psalm 101:2–6

WEEK 15

BEING HONEST

Weekend

Help, LORD, for the godly are no more;
  the faithful have vanished from among men.
Everyone lies to his neighbor;
  their flattering lips speak with deception.

May the LORD cut off all flattering lips
  and every boastful tongue
that says, "We will triumph with our tongues;
  we own our lips—who is our master?"

"Because of the oppression of the weak
  and the groaning of the needy,
I will now arise," says the LORD.
  "I will protect them from those who
malign them."
And the words of the LORD are flawless,
  like silver refined in a furnace of clay,
  purified seven times.
O LORD, you will keep us safe
  and protect us from such people forever.

—Psalm 12:1–7

CONCERN FOR THE FUTURE

Monday

CONSIDER WHAT GOD HAS DONE:
Who can straighten
  what he has made crooked?
When times are good, be happy;
  but when times are bad, consider:
God has made the one
  as well as the other.
Therefore, a man cannot discover
  anything about his future.

—Ecclesiastes 7:13–14

"**F**or I know the plans I have for you," declares
the LORD, "plans to prosper you and not to harm
you, plans to give you hope and a future. Then
you will call upon me and come and pray to me,
and I will listen to you."

—Jeremiah 29:11–12

Tell the righteous *it will be well with them,*
  for they will enjoy the fruit of their deeds.

—Isaiah 3:10

CONCERN FOR THE FUTURE

Tuesday

Wait for the LORD
  and keep his way.
He will exalt you to inherit the land;
  when the wicked are cut off, you will see it.

I have seen a wicked and ruthless man
  flourishing like a green tree in its native soil,
but he soon passed away and was no more;
  though I looked for him, he could not be
found.

Consider the blameless, observe the upright;
  there is a future for the man of peace.

—Psalm 37:34–37

Do not let your heart envy sinners,
  but always be zealous for the fear of the LORD.
There is surely a future hope for you,
  and your hope will not be cut off.

—Proverbs 23:17–18

Wednesday

Since no man knows the future,
  who can tell him what is to come?
No man has power over the wind to contain it;
  so no one has power over the day of his death.

—**Ecclesiastes 8:7–8**

I trust in you, O LORD;
  I say, "You are my God."
My times are in your hands.

—**Psalm 31:14–15**

Listen, you who say, "Today or tomorrow we will go to this or that city, spend a year there, carry on business and make money." Why, you do not even know what will happen tomorrow. What is your life? You are a mist that appears for a little while and then vanishes. Instead, you ought to say, "If it is the LORD's will, we will live and do this or that."

—**James 4:13–15**

Thursday

Where can I go from your Spirit?
 Where can I flee from your presence?
If I go up to the heavens, you are there;
 if I make my bed in the depths, you are there.
If I rise on the wings of the dawn,
 if I settle on the far side of the sea,
even there your hand will guide me,
 your right hand will hold me fast....
For you created my inmost being;
 you knit me together in my mother's womb.
I praise you because I am fearfully and
wonderfully made....
My frame was not hidden from you
 when I was made in the secret place.
When I was woven together in the depths of
the earth,
 your eyes saw my unformed body.

All the days ordained for me
 were written in your book
 before one of them came to be.

—Psalm 139:7–10, 13–16

CONCERN FOR THE FUTURE

Friday

The fear of the LORD adds length to life,
  but the years of the wicked are cut short.

—Proverbs 10:27

In the house of the wise are stores of choice
food and oil,
  but a foolish man devours all he has.

—Proverbs 21:20

The race is not to the swift
  or the battle to the strong,
nor does food come to the wise
  or wealth to the brilliant
  or favor to the learned;
but time and chance happen to them all.

—Ecclesiastes 9:11

Do not boast about tomorrow
  for you do not know what a day may
bring forth.

—Proverbs 27:1

CONCERN FOR THE FUTURE

Weekend

*Trust in the L*ORD *with all your heart*
  and lean not on your own understanding;
in all your ways acknowledge him,
  and he will make your paths straight.

—Proverbs 3:5–6

THIS IS WHAT THE LORD **SAYS:**
"Restrain your voice from weeping
  and your eyes from tears,
for your work will be rewarded,"
    declares the LORD.
"...There is hope for your future,"
    declares the LORD.

—Jeremiah 31:16–17

OVERCOMING FEAR

Monday

"**B**e *strong and courageous. Do not be afraid* or terrified because of them, for the LORD your God goes with you; he will never leave you nor forsake you."
Then Moses summoned Joshua and said to him in the presence of all Israel, "Be strong and courageous, for you must go with this people into the land that the LORD swore to their forefathers to give them, and you must divide it among them as their inheritance. The LORD himself goes before you and will be with you; he will never leave you nor forsake you."

—**Deuteronomy 31:6–8**

He who dwells in the shelter of the Most High
    will rest in the shadow of the Almighty.
I will say of the LORD, "He is my refuge and
my fortress,
    my God, in whom I trust."

—**Psalm 91:1–2**

Tuesday

GOD HAS SAID,
"Never will I leave you;
never will I forsake you."

So we say with confidence,
"The LORD is my helper; I will not be afraid.
What can man do to me?"

—Hebrews 13:5–6

Those who are led by the Spirit of God are sons of God. For you did not receive a spirit that makes you a slave again to fear, but you received the Spirit of sonship. And by him we cry, "Abba, Father." The Spirit himself testifies with our spirit that we are God's children. We are heirs ... of God and coheirs with Christ, if indeed we share in his sufferings in order that we may also share in his glory.

—Romans 8:14–17

Wednesday

"**S**urely God is my salvation;
   I will trust and not be afraid.
The LORD, the LORD, is my strength and
my song;
   he has become my salvation."

—Isaiah 12:2

For God did not give us a spirit of timidity, but
a spirit of power, of love and of self-discipline.

—2 Timothy 1:7

When I am afraid,
   I will trust in you.
In God, whose word I praise,
   in God I trust; I will not be afraid.
   What can mortal man do to me?

—Psalm 56:3–4

OVERCOMING FEAR

Thursday

One thing I ask of the LORD,
    this is what I seek:
that I may dwell in the house of the LORD
    all the days of my life,
to gaze upon the beauty of the LORD
    and to seek him in his temple.
For in the day of trouble
    he will keep me safe in his dwelling;
he will hide me in the shelter of his tabernacle
    and set me high upon a rock.
Then my head will be exalted
    above the enemies who surround me;
at his tabernacle will I sacrifice with shouts
of joy;
    I will sing and make music to the LORD.

—Psalm 27:4–6

Friday

Peace I leave with you; my peace I give you. I do not give to you as the world gives. Do not let your hearts be troubled and do not be afraid.

—John 14:27

My enemies will turn back
  when I call for help.
  By this I will know that God is for me.
In God, whose word I praise,
  in the LORD, whose word I praise—
in God I trust; I will not be afraid.
  What can man do to me?

—Psalm 56:9–11

God is love. Whoever lives in love lives in God, and God in him. In this way, love is made complete among us so that we will have confidence on the day of judgment, because in this world we are like him. There is no fear in love. But perfect love drives out fear, because fear has to do with punishment. The one who fears is not made perfect in love.

—1 John 4:16–18

Weekend

The word of the LORD came to [Jeremiah], saying,

"Before I formed you in the womb I knew you,
before you were born I set you apart;
I appointed you as a prophet to the nations."

"Ah, Sovereign LORD," he said, "I do not know how to speak; I am only a child."
But the LORD said to him, "Do not say, 'I am only a child.' You must go to everyone I send you to and say whatever I command you. Do not be afraid of them, for I am with you and will rescue you," declares the LORD.

—Jeremiah 1:4–8

The LORD is with me; I will not be afraid.
What can man do to me?
The LORD is with me; he is my helper.
I will look in triumph on my enemies.

—Psalm 118:6–7

RESISTING CHEATING

Monday

Honest scales and balances are from the LORD;
all the weights in the bag are of his making.

—**Proverbs 16:11**

Do not have two differing weights in your bag—
one heavy, one light. Do not have two differing
measures in your house—one large, one small.
You must have accurate and honest weights and
measures, so that you may live long in the land
the LORD your God is giving you. For the LORD
your God detests anyone who does these things,
anyone who deals dishonestly.

—**Deuteronomy 25:13–16**

For the company of the godless will be barren,
and fire will consume the tents of those who
love bribes.

—**Job 15:34**

The integrity of the upright guides them,
but the unfaithful are destroyed by
their duplicity.

—**Proverbs 11:3**

Tuesday

See to it, brothers, that none of you has a sinful, unbelieving heart that turns away from the living God. But encourage one another daily, as long as it is called Today, so that none of you may be hardened by sin's deceitfulness.

—Hebrews 3:12–13

"**T**wo things I ask of you, O LORD;
   do not refuse me before I die:
Keep falsehood and lies far from me;
   give me neither poverty nor riches,
   but give me only my daily bread.
Otherwise, I may have too much and
disown you
   and say, 'Who is the LORD?'
Or I may become poor and steal,
   and so dishonor the name of my God."

—Proverbs 30:7–9

RESISTING CHEATING

Wednesday

"**W**hoever can be trusted with very little can also be trusted with much, and whoever is dishonest with very little will also be dishonest with much. So if you have not been trustworthy in handling worldly wealth, who will trust you with true riches? And if you have not been trustworthy with someone else's property, who will give you property of your own?

"No servant can serve two masters. Either he will hate the one and love the other, or he will be devoted to the one and despise the other. You cannot serve both God and Money."

—Luke 16:10–13

Follow justice and justice alone, so that you may live and possess the land the LORD your God is giving you.

—Deuteronomy 16:20

Thursday

Do not trust in extortion
   or take pride in stolen goods;
though your riches increase,
   do not set your heart on them.

—Psalm 62:10

This is what the LORD says:

"Maintain justice
   and do what is right,
for my salvation is close at hand
   and my righteousness will soon be revealed."

—Isaiah 56:1

The LORD abhors dishonest scales,
but accurate weights are his delight.

—Proverbs 11:1

RESISTING CHEATING

Friday

Zacchaeus stood up and said to the LORD, "Look, LORD! Here and now I give half of my possessions to the poor, and if I have cheated anybody out of anything, I will pay back four times the amount." Jesus said to him, "Today salvation has come to this house, because this man, too, is a son of Abraham. For the Son of Man came to seek and to save what was lost."

—Luke 19:8–10

Samuel said to all Israel, "I have listened to everything you said to me and have set a king over you. Now you have a king as your leader.... I have been your leader from my youth until this day. Here I stand. Testify against me in the presence of the LORD and his anointed. Whose ox have I taken? Whose donkey have I taken? Whom have I cheated? Whom have I oppressed? From whose hand have I accepted a bribe to make me shut my eyes? If I have done any of these, I will make it right."

—1 Samuel 12:1–3

RESISTING CHEATING

Weekend

Hear this, you who trample the needy
   and do away with the poor of the land,

saying,

"When will the New Moon be over
   that we may sell grain,
and the Sabbath be ended
   that we may market wheat?"—
skimping the measure,
   boosting the price
   and cheating with dishonest scales,
buying the poor with silver
   and the needy for a pair of sandals,
   selling even the sweepings with the wheat.

The LORD has sworn by the Pride of Jacob: "I will
never forget anything they have done."

—**Amos 8:4–7**

THE VALUE OF INSTRUCTION

Monday

Wisdom has built her house;
   she has hewn out its seven pillars.
She has prepared her meat and mixed
her wine;
   she has also set her table.
She has sent out her maids, and she calls ...
"Let all who are simple come in here!"
   she says to those who lack judgment.
"Come, eat my food
   and drink the wine I have mixed.
Leave your simple ways and you will live;
   walk in the way of understanding."

—Proverbs 9:1–6

"**R**emember the instruction you gave your servant Moses, saying, 'If you are unfaithful, I will
scatter you among the nations, but if you return to
me and obey my commands, then even if your
exiled people are at the farthest horizon, I will
gather them from there and bring them to the
place I have chosen as a dwelling for my Name.' "

—Nehemiah 1:8–9

Tuesday

"Submit to God and be at peace with him;
  in this way prosperity will come to you.
Accept instruction from his mouth
  and lay up his words in your heart.
If you return to the Almighty, you will be restored:
  If you remove wickedness far from your tent
and assign your nuggets to the dust,
  your gold of Ophir to the rocks in the ravines,
then the Almighty will be your gold,
  the choicest silver for you.
You will pray to him, and he will hear you,
  and you will fulfill your vows.
What you decide on will be done,
  and light will shine on your ways.
When men are brought low and you say, 'Lift
them up!'
  then he will save the downcast.
He will deliver even one who is not innocent,
  who will be delivered through the cleanness
of your hands."

—Job 22:21–25, 27–30

THE VALUE OF INSTRUCTION

Wednesday

Do good to your servant, and I will live;
  I will obey your word.
Open my eyes that I may see
  wonderful things in your law.
I am a stranger on earth;
  do not hide your commands from me.
My soul is consumed with longing
  for your laws at all times.
You rebuke the arrogant, who are cursed
  and who stray from your commands.
Remove from me scorn and contempt,
  for I keep your statutes.
Though rulers sit together and slander me,
  your servant will meditate on your decrees.
Your statutes are my delight;
  they are my counselors.

—Psalm 119:17–24

Stop listening to instruction, my son,
  and you will stray from the words
of knowledge.

—Proverbs 19:27

THE VALUE OF INSTRUCTION

Thursday

"**Y**ou will know that I have sent you this admonition so that my covenant with Levi may continue," says the LORD Almighty. "My covenant was with him, a covenant of life and peace, and I gave them to him; this called for reverence and he revered me and stood in awe of my name. True instruction was in his mouth and nothing false was found on his lips. He walked with me in peace and uprightness, and turned many from sin.

"For the lips of a priest ought to preserve knowledge, and from his mouth men should seek instruction—because he is the messenger of the LORD Almighty. But you have turned from the way and by your teaching have caused many to stumble; you have violated the covenant with Levi," says the LORD Almighty. "So I have caused you to be despised and humiliated before all the people, because you have not followed my ways but have shown partiality in matters of the law."

—Malachi 2:4–9

THE VALUE OF INSTRUCTION

Friday

All your commands are trustworthy;
    help me, for men persecute me without cause.
They almost wiped me from the earth,
    but I have not forsaken your precepts.
Preserve my life according to your love,
    and I will obey the statutes of your mouth.

—**Psalm 119:86–88**

The lips of the wise spread knowledge;
    not so the hearts of fools.

—**Proverbs 15:7**

The quiet words of the wise are more to
be heeded
    than the shouts of a ruler of fools.
Wisdom is better than weapons of war,
    but one sinner destroys much good.

—**Ecclesiastes 9:17–18**

Weekend

Hear the word of the LORD, you Israelites,
    because the LORD has a charge to bring
    against you who live in the land:
"There is no faithfulness, no love,
    no acknowledgment of God in the land.
There is only cursing, lying and murder,
    stealing and adultery;
they break all bounds,
    and bloodshed follows bloodshed.
Because of this the land mourns,
    and all who live in it waste away....
"You stumble day and night,
    and the prophets stumble with you.
So I will destroy your mother—
    my people are destroyed from lack
of knowledge.

"Because you have rejected knowledge,
    I also reject you as my priests;
because you have ignored the law of your God,
    I also will ignore your children."

—Hosea 4:1–3, 5–6

Monday

I ask that we love one another. And this is love: that we walk in obedience to his commands. As you have heard from the beginning, his command is that you walk in love.

—2 John 5–6

We who are strong ought to bear with the failings of the weak and not to please ourselves. Each of us should please his neighbor for his good, to build him up. For even Christ did not please himself but, as it is written: "The insults of those who insult you have fallen on me." For everything that was written in the past was written to teach us, so that through endurance and the encouragement of the Scriptures we might have hope.

—Romans 15:1–4

Many a man claims to
    have unfailing love,
but a faithful man who
    can find?

—Proverbs 20:6

Tuesday

In Christ Jesus ... the only thing that counts is faith expressing itself through love.

—**Galatians 5:6**

This is how we know what love is: Jesus Christ laid down his life for us. And we ought to lay down our lives for our brothers. If anyone has material possessions and sees his brother in need but has no pity on him, how can the love of God *be in him?*

—1 John 3:16–17

We love because [God] first loved us. If anyone says, "I love God," yet hates his brother, he is a liar. For anyone who does not love his brother, whom he has seen, cannot love God, whom he has not seen. And he has given us this command: Whoever loves God must also love his brother.

—1 John 4:19–21

BEING A TRUE FRIEND

Wednesday

Live in peace with each other. And we urge you, brothers, warn those who are idle, encourage the timid, help the weak, be patient with everyone. Make sure that nobody pays back wrong for wrong, but always try to be kind to each other and to everyone else.

—1 Thessalonians 5:13–15

Dear children, let us not love with words or tongue but with actions and in truth.

—1 John 3:18

One of [the Pharisees], an expert in the law, [asked Jesus]:
"Teacher, which is the greatest commandment in the Law?" Jesus replied: " 'Love the LORD your God with all your heart and with all your soul and with all your mind.' This is the first and greatest commandment. And the second is like it: 'Love your neighbor as yourself.' All the Law and the Prophets hang on these two commandments."

—Matthew 22:35–40

Thursday

Do nothing out of selfish ambition or vain conceit, but in humility consider others better than yourselves. Each of you should look not only to your own interests, but also to the interests of others.

—**Philippians 2:3–4**

Carry each other's burdens, and in this way you will fulfill the law of Christ.

—**Galatians 6:2**

JOHN THE BAPTIST SAID:
"You yourselves can testify that I said, 'I am not the Christ but am sent ahead of him.' The bride belongs to the bridegroom. The friend who attends the bridegroom waits and listens for him, and is full of joy when he hears the bridegroom's voice. That joy is mine, and it is now complete. He must become greater; I must become less."

—**John 3:28–30**

Friday

Love must be sincere. Hate what is evil; cling to what is good. Be devoted to one another in brotherly love. Honor one another above yourselves.... Share with God's people who are in need. Practice hospitality.

Bless those who persecute you; bless and do not curse. Rejoice with those who rejoice; mourn with those who mourn. Live in harmony with one another.

—**Romans 12:9–10, 13–16**

*Like one who takes away a garment on a
cold day,*
    or like vinegar poured on soda,
    is one who sings songs to a heavy heart.

—**Proverbs 25:20**

*The purposes of a man's heart are deep waters,
    but a man of understanding draws them out.*

—**Proverbs 20:5**

Weekend

Do not forsake your friend and the friend of your father.

—Proverbs 27:10

Ruth replied, "Don't urge me to leave you or to turn back from you. Where you go I will go, and where you stay I will stay. Your people will be my people and your God my God. Where you die I will die, and there I will be buried. May the LORD deal with me, be it ever so severely, if anything but death separates you and me."

—Ruth 1:16–17

Praise be to the God and Father of our LORD Jesus Christ, the Father of compassion and the God of all comfort, who comforts us in all our troubles, so that we can comfort those in any trouble with the comfort we ourselves have received from God.

—2 Corinthians 1:3–4

Monday

My dear brothers, take note of this: Everyone should be quick to listen, slow to speak and slow to become angry.

—James 1:19

The LORD said to [Jeremiah], "Proclaim all these words in the towns of Judah and in the streets of Jerusalem: 'Listen to the terms of this covenant and follow them. From the time I brought your forefathers up from Egypt until today, I warned them again and again, saying, "Obey me." But they did not listen or pay attention; instead, they followed the stubbornness of their evil hearts. So I brought on them all the curses of the covenant I had commanded them to follow but that they did not keep.' "

—Jeremiah 11:6–8

The more the words,
the less the meaning,
and how does that profit anyone?

—Ecclesiastes 6:11

Tuesday

He who answers before listening—
that is his folly and his shame.

—Proverbs 18:13

Do not merely listen to the word, and so deceive yourselves. Do what it says. Anyone who listens to the word but does not do what it says is like a man who looks at his face in a mirror and, after looking at himself, goes away and immediately forgets what he looks like. But the man who looks intently into the perfect law that gives freedom, and continues to do this, not forgetting what he has heard, but doing it—he will be blessed in what he does.

If anyone considers himself religious and yet does not keep a tight rein on his tongue, he deceives himself and his religion is worthless.

—James 1:22–26

He who guards his lips guards his life,
but he who speaks rashly will come to ruin.

—Proverbs 13:3

Wednesday

[At Marah] the LORD made a decree and a law for [the Israelites], and there he tested them. He said, "If you listen carefully to the voice of the LORD your God and do what is right in his eyes, if you pay attention to his commands and keep all his decrees, I will not bring on you any of the diseases I brought on the Egyptians, for I am the LORD, who heals you."

—**Exodus 15:25–26**

Apply your heart to instruction
and your ears to words of knowledge.

—**Proverbs 23:12**

JEREMIAH SAID OF THE ISRAELITES:
To whom can I speak and give warning?
Who will listen to me?
Their ears are closed
so they cannot hear.
The word of the LORD is offensive to them;
they find no pleasure in it.

—**Jeremiah 6:10**

Thursday

When words are many, sin is not absent,
  but he who holds his tongue is wise.

—**Proverbs 10:19**

IN HIS COVENANT WITH ISRAEL
THE LORD SAID:
"See, I am sending an angel ahead of you to
guard you along the way and to bring you to the
place I have prepared. Pay attention to him and
listen to what he says. Do not rebel against him;
he will not forgive your rebellion, since my Name
is in him. If you listen carefully to what he says
and do all that I say, I will be an enemy to your
enemies and will oppose those who oppose you."

—**Exodus 23:20–22**

The wise in heart accept commands,
  but a chattering fool comes to ruin.

—**Proverbs 10:8**

THE IMPORTANCE OF LISTENING

Friday

Even a fool is thought wise if he keeps silent,
  and discerning if he holds his tongue.

—**Proverbs 17:28**

ONE OF JOB'S FRIENDS PLEADED
WITH HIM:
"Pay attention, Job, and listen to me;
  be silent, and I will speak.
If you have anything to say, answer me;
  speak up, for I want you to be cleared.
But if not, then listen to me;
  be silent, and I will teach you wisdom."

—**Job 33:31–33**

Set a guard over my mouth, O LORD;
keep watch over the door of my lips.

—**Psalm 141:3**

THE IMPORTANCE OF LISTENING

Weekend

Do you see a man who speaks in haste?
  There is more hope for a fool than for him.

—**Proverbs 29:20**

THEN JOB REPLIED TO THE LORD:
"I know that you can do all things;
  no plan of yours can be thwarted.
You asked, 'Who is this that obscures my counsel
without knowledge?'
  Surely I spoke of things I did not understand,
  things too wonderful for me to know.

"You said, 'Listen now, and I will speak;
  I will question you,
  and you shall answer me.'
My ears had heard of you
  but now my eyes have seen you.
Therefore I despise myself
  and repent in dust and ashes."

—**Job 42:1–6**

BEING DISCIPLINED

Monday

My son, do not despise the LORD's discipline
    and do not resent his rebuke,
because the LORD disciplines those he loves,
    as a father the son he delights in.

—**Proverbs 3:11–12**

He will die for lack of discipline,
    led astray by his own great folly.

—**Proverbs 5:23**

Blessed is the man you discipline, O LORD,
    the man you teach from your law;
you grant him relief from days of trouble,
    till a pit is dug for the wicked.
For the LORD will not reject his people;
    he will never forsake his inheritance.
Judgment will again be founded
on righteousness,
    and all the upright in heart will follow it.

—**Psalm 94:12–15**

Tuesday

Be *self-controlled and alert.*

—1 Peter 5:8

But the day of the LORD will come like a thief. The heavens will disappear with a roar; the elements will be destroyed by fire, and the earth and everything in it will be laid bare.

Since everything will be destroyed in this way, what kind of people ought you to be? You ought to live holy and godly lives as you look forward to the day of God and speed its coming. That day will bring about the destruction of the heavens by fire, and the elements will melt in the heat. But in keeping with his promise we are looking forward to a new heaven and a new earth, the home of righteousness.

So then, dear friends, since you are looking forward to this, make every effort to be found spotless, blameless and at peace with him.

—2 Peter 3:10–14

BEING DISCIPLINED

Wednesday

Seek good, not evil,
that you may live.
Then the LORD God Almighty will be with you,
just as you say he is.
Hate evil, love good;
maintain justice in the courts.

—Amos 5:14–15

He who heeds discipline shows the way to life,
but whoever ignores correction leads
others astray.

—Proverbs 10:17

He who ignores discipline despises himself,
but whoever heeds correction
gains understanding.

—Proverbs 15:32

Thursday

In your struggle against sin, you have not yet resisted to the point of shedding your blood. And you have forgotten that word of encouragement that addresses you as sons:

*"My son, do not make light of the
LORD's discipline,
    and do not lose heart when he rebukes you,
because the LORD disciplines those he loves,
    and he punishes everyone he accepts as
a son."*

Endure hardship as discipline; God is treating you as sons. For what son is not disciplined by his father? We have all had human fathers who disciplined us and we respected them for it. How much more should we submit to the Father of our spirits and live! … God disciplines us for our good, that we may share in his holiness. No discipline seems pleasant at the time, but painful. Later on, however, it produces a harvest of righteousness and peace for those who have been trained by it."

—Hebrews 12:4–7, 9–13

BEING DISCIPLINED

Friday

My son, keep your father's commands
 and do not forsake your mother's teaching.
Bind them upon your heart forever;
 fasten them around your neck.
When you walk, they will guide you;
 when you sleep, they will watch over you;
 when you awake, they will speak to you.
For these commands are a lamp,
 his teaching is a light,
and the corrections of discipline
 are the way to life.

—**Proverbs 6:20–23**

MOSES REMINDED THE ISRAELITES:
[The LORD] humbled you, causing you to hunger
and then feeding you with manna, ... to teach
you that man does not live on bread alone but on
every word that comes from the mouth of the
LORD. Your clothes did not wear out and your feet
did not swell during these forty years. Know then
in your heart that as a man disciplines his son,
so the LORD your God disciplines you.

—**Deuteronomy 8:3–5**

BEING DISCIPLINED

Weekend

THE PROVERBS OF SOLOMON SON
OF DAVID, KING OF ISRAEL:
for attaining wisdom and discipline;
  for understanding words of insight;
for acquiring a disciplined and prudent life,
  doing what is right and just and fair;
for giving prudence to the simple,
  knowledge and discretion to the young—
let the wise listen and add to their learning,
  and let the discerning get guidance—
for understanding proverbs and parables,
  the sayings and riddles of the wise.

—**Proverbs 1:1–6**

JESUS SAID:
"Those whom I love I rebuke and discipline. So
be earnest, and repent. Here I am! I stand at the
door and knock. If anyone hears my voice and
opens the door, I will come in and eat with him,
and he with me. To him who overcomes, I will
give the right to sit with me on my throne...."

—**Revelation 3:19–21**

STAYING POSITIVE

Monday

The LORD said to Moses, "Send some men to explore the land of Canaan, which I am giving to the Israelites...." So at the LORD's command Moses sent them out.... At the end of forty days they ... gave Moses this account: "The people who live there are powerful, and the cities are fortified and very large...." Then Caleb ... said, "We should go up and take possession of the land, for we can certainly do it." But the men who had gone up with him said, "We can't attack those people; they are stronger than we are." And they spread among the Israelites a bad report about the land they had explored.... All the Israelites grumbled against Moses and Aaron, ...the whole assembly talked about stoning them.... The LORD said to Moses, ... "No one who has treated me with contempt will ever see [the land]. But because my servant Caleb has a different spirit and follows me wholeheartedly, I will bring him into the land he went to, and his descendants will inherit it."

—**Numbers 13:1–3, 25, 27–28,
30–32; 14:2, 10, 23–24**

Tuesday

Now the people complained about their hardships in the hearing of the LORD, and when he heard them his anger was aroused. Then fire from the LORD burned among them and consumed some of the outskirts of the camp. When the people cried out to Moses, he prayed to the LORD and the fire died down. So that place was called Taberah, because fire from the LORD had burned among them.

—**Numbers 11:1–3**

Do everything without complaining or arguing, so that you may become blameless and pure, children of God without fault in a crooked and depraved generation, in which you shine like stars in the universe.

—**Philippians 2:14–15**

Devote yourselves to prayer, *being watchful and thankful.*

—**Colossians 4:2**

STAYING POSITIVE

Wednesday

As the deer pants for streams of water,
  so my soul pants for you, O God.
My soul thirsts for God, for the living God.
  When can I go and meet with God?
My tears have been my food
  day and night,
while men say to me all day long,
  "Where is your God?"
These things I remember
  as I pour out my soul:
how I used to go with the multitude,
  leading the procession to the house of God,
with shouts of joy and thanksgiving
  among the festive throng.

Why are you downcast, O my soul?
  Why so disturbed within me?
Put your hope in God,
  for I will yet praise him,
  my Savior and my God.

—Psalm 42:1–6

Thursday

Lift your eyes and look to the heavens:
  Who created all these?
He who brings out the starry host one by one,
  and calls them each by name.
Because of his great power and mighty strength,
  not one of them is missing.

Why do you say, O Jacob,
and complain, O Israel,
"My way is hidden from the LORD;
my cause is disregarded by my God"?

—**Isaiah 40:26–27**

I have learned to be content whatever the circumstances. I know what it is to be in need, and I know what it is to have plenty. I have learned the secret of being content in any and every situation, whether well fed or hungry, whether living in plenty or in want. I can do everything through him who gives me strength.

—**Philippians 4:11–13**

STAYING POSITIVE

Friday.

Who can speak and have it happen
    if the LORD has not decreed it?
Is it not from the mouth of the Most High
    that both calamities and good things come?
Why should any living man complain
    when punished for his sins?

Let us examine our ways and test them,
    and let us return to the LORD.

—**Lamentations 3:37–40**

The fear of the LORD leads to life:
    Then one rests content, untouched by trouble.

—**Proverbs 19:23**

Godliness with contentment is great gain. For
we brought nothing into the world, and we can
take nothing out of it. But if we have food and
clothing, we will be content with that.

—**1 Timothy 6:6–8**

STAYING POSITIVE

Weekend

I cry aloud to the LORD;
  I lift up my voice to the LORD for mercy.
I pour out my complaint before him;
  before him I tell my trouble.

When my spirit grows faint within me,
  it is you who know my way....
I cry to you, O LORD;
  I say, "You are my refuge,
  my portion in the land of the living."
Listen to my cry,
  for I am in desperate need;
rescue me from those who pursue me,
  for they are too strong for me.
Set me free from my prison,
  that I may praise your name.

Then the righteous will gather about me
  because of your goodness to me.

—Psalm 142:1–3, 5–7

NOT GIVING UP

Monday

Let us not become weary in doing good, for at the proper time we will reap a harvest if we do not give up. Therefore, as we have opportunity, let us do good to all people, especially to those who belong to the family of believers.

—**Galatians 6:9–10**

Blessed is the man who perseveres under trial, because when he has stood the test, he will receive the crown of life that God has promised to those who love him.

—**James 1:12**

"Let us acknowledge the LORD;
    let us press on to acknowledge him.
As surely as the sun rises,
    he will appear;
he will come to us like the winter rains,
    like the spring rains that water the earth."

—**Hosea 6:3**

NOT GIVING UP

Tuesday

JESUS TOLD THIS PARABLE:
"A farmer went out to sow his seed. As he was scattering the seed, some fell ... on good soil. It came up and yielded a crop, a hundred times more than was sown." ... The seed on good soil stands for those with a noble and good heart, who hear the word, retain it, and by persevering produce a crop.

—Luke 8:5, 8, 15

Paul writes, about the message of the gospel:
We have this treasure in jars of clay to show that this all-surpassing power is from God and not from us. We are hard pressed on every side, but not crushed; perplexed, but not in despair; persecuted, but not abandoned; struck down, but not destroyed.

—2 Corinthians 4:7–9

Wednesday

Consider it pure joy, my brothers, whenever you face trials of many kinds, because you know that the testing of your faith develops perseverance. Perseverance must finish its work so that you may be mature and complete, not lacking anything.

—James 1:2–4

I will exalt you, O LORD,
　　for you lifted me out of the depths
　　and did not let my enemies gloat over me.
O LORD my God, I called to you for help
　　and you healed me.
O LORD, you brought me up from the grave;
　　you spared me from going down into the pit.

Sing to the LORD, you saints of his;
　　praise his holy name.
For his anger lasts only a moment,
　　but his favor lasts a lifetime;
weeping may remain for a night,
　　but rejoicing comes in the morning.

—Psalm 30:1–5

Thursday

Do not throw away your confidence; it will be richly rewarded. You need to persevere so that when you have done the will of God, you will receive what he has promised. For in just a very *little while,*

"He who is coming will come and will not delay.
But my righteous one will live by faith.
And if he shrinks back,
I will not be pleased with him."

But we are not of those who shrink back and are destroyed, but of those who believe and are saved.

—Hebrews 10:35–39

Friday

I know your deeds, your hard work and your perseverance. I know that you cannot tolerate wicked men, that you have tested those who claim to be apostles but are not, and have found them false. You have persevered and have endured hardships for my name, and have not grown weary.

—**Revelation 2:2–3**

And we pray this in order that you may live a life worthy of the LORD and may please him in every way: bearing fruit in every good work, growing in the knowledge of God, being strengthened with all power according to his glorious might so that you may have great endurance and patience, and joyfully giving thanks to the Father, who has qualified you to share in the inheritance of the saints in the kingdom of light.

—**Colossians 1:10–12**

Weekend

Turn to me and be gracious to me,
    for I am lonely and afflicted.
The troubles of my heart have multiplied;
    free me from my anguish.
Look upon my affliction and my distress
    and take away all my sins.
See how my enemies have increased
    and how fiercely they hate me!
Guard my life and rescue me;
    let me not be put to shame,
    for I take refuge in you.
May integrity and uprightness protect me,
    because my hope is in you.

—**Psalm 25:16–21**

We rejoice in our sufferings, because we know that suffering produces perseverance; perseverance, character; and character, hope. And hope does not disappoint us, because God has poured out his love into our hearts by the Holy Spirit, whom he has given us.

—**Romans 5:3–5**

AVOIDING FIGHTS AND ARGUMENTS

Monday

What causes fights and quarrels among you? Don't they come from your desires that battle within you? You want something but don't get it. You kill and covet, but you cannot have what you want. You quarrel and fight. You do not have, because you do not ask God. When you ask, you do not receive, because you ask with wrong motives, that you may spend what you get on your pleasures.

—James 4:1–3

A greedy man stirs up dissension,
  but he who trusts in the LORD will prosper.

—Proverbs 28:25

Judgment without mercy will be shown to anyone who has not been merciful. Mercy triumphs over judgment!

—James 2:13

It is to a man's honor to avoid strife,
  but every fool is quick to quarrel.

—Proverbs 20:3

Tuesday

JESUS SAID:

"You have heard that it was said, 'Love your neighbor and hate your enemy.' But I tell you: Love your enemies and pray for those who persecute you, that you may be sons of your Father in heaven. He causes his sun to rise on the evil and the good, and sends rain on the righteous and the unrighteous. If you love those who love you, what reward will you get? Are not even the tax collectors doing that? And if you greet only your brothers, what are you doing more than others? Do not even pagans do that?"

—**Matthew 5:43–47**

May the God who gives endurance and encouragement give you a spirit of unity among yourselves as you follow Christ Jesus, so that with one heart and mouth you may glorify the God and Father of our LORD Jesus Christ.

—**Romans 15:5–6**

Wednesday

There are six things the LORD hates,
    seven that are detestable to him:
        haughty eyes,
        a lying tongue,
        hands that shed innocent blood,
        a heart that devises wicked schemes,
        feet that are quick to rush into evil,
        a false witness who pours out lies
        and a man who stirs up dissension
among brothers.

—**Proverbs 6:16–19**

Hatred stirs up dissension,
    but love covers over all wrongs.

—**Proverbs 10:12**

In your anger do not sin;
    when you are on your beds,
    search your hearts and be silent.

—**Psalm 4:4**

AVOIDING FIGHTS AND ARGUMENTS

Thursday

An angry man stirs up dissension,
and a hot-tempered one commits many sins.

—Proverbs 29:22

JESUS SAID:
"You have heard that it was said, 'Eye for eye,
and tooth for tooth.' But I tell you, Do not resist an
evil person. If someone strikes you on the right
cheek, turn to him the other also. And if someone
wants to sue you and take your tunic, let him
have your cloak as well. If someone forces you to
go one mile, go with him two miles. Give to the
one who asks you, and do not turn away from
the one who wants to borrow from you."

—Matthew 5:38–42

A man's wisdom gives him patience;
it is to his glory to overlook an offense.

—Proverbs 19:11

AVOIDING FIGHTS AND ARGUMENTS

Friday

Do not repay anyone evil for evil. Be careful to do what is right in the eyes of everybody. If it is possible, as far as it depends on you, live at peace with everyone. Do not take revenge, my friends, but leave room for God's wrath, for it is written: "It is mine to avenge; I will repay," says the LORD. On the contrary:

"If your enemy is hungry, feed him;
  if he is thirsty, give him something to drink.
In doing this, you will heap burning coals on
his head."

Do not be overcome by evil, but overcome evil with good.

—Romans 12:17–21

"The LORD is slow to anger, abounding in love and forgiving sin and rebellion. Yet he does not leave the guilty unpunished."

—Numbers 14:18

Weekend

JESUS SAID:

"You have heard that it was said to the people long ago, 'Do not murder, and anyone who murders will be subject to judgment.' But I tell you that anyone who is angry with his brother will be subject to judgment. Again, anyone who says to his brother, 'Raca,' is answerable to the Sanhedrin. But anyone who says, 'You fool!' will be in danger of the fire of hell. Therefore if you are offering your gift at the altar and there remember that your brother has something against you, leave your gift there in front of the altar. First go and be reconciled to your brother; then come and offer your gift."

—Matthew 5:21–24

The commandments... are summed up in this one rule: "Love your neighbor as yourself." Love does no harm to its neighbor. Therefore, love is the fulfillment of the law."

—Romans 13:9–10

GUARDING YOUR HEALTH

Monday

Do not be wise in your own eyes;
  fear the LORD and shun evil.
This will bring health to your body
  and nourishment to your bones.

—Proverbs 3:7–8

My son, pay attention to what I say;
  listen closely to my words.
Do not let them out of your sight,
  keep them within your heart;
for they are life to those who find them
  and health to a man's whole body.
Above all else, guard your heart,
  for it is the wellspring of life.

—Proverbs 4:20–23

[The LORD] heals the brokenhearted
and binds up their wounds.

—Psalm 147:3

Tuesday

A *heart at peace gives life to the body,*
but envy rots the bones.

—**Proverbs 14:30**

A *cheerful look brings joy to the heart,*
and good news gives health to the bones.

—**Proverbs 15:30**

A *cheerful heart is good medicine,*
but a crushed spirit dries up the bones.

—**Proverbs 17:22**

P*leasant words are a honeycomb,*
sweet to the soul and healing to the bones.

—**Proverbs 16:24**

GUARDING YOUR HEALTH

Wednesday

A man's spirit sustains him in sickness,
   but a crushed spirit who can bear?

—Proverbs 18:14

Praise the LORD, O my soul;
   all my inmost being, praise his holy name.
Praise the LORD, O my soul,
   and forget not all his benefits—
who forgives all your sins
   and heals all your diseases,
who redeems your life from the pit
   and crowns you with love and compassion,
who satisfies your desires with good things
   so that your youth is renewed like the eagle's.

—Psalm 103:1–5

GUARDING YOUR HEALTH

Thursday

Jesus went through all the towns and villages, teaching in their synagogues, preaching the good news of the kingdom and healing every disease and sickness.

—**Matthew 9:35**

Jesus Christ is the same yesterday and today and forever.

—**Hebrews 13:8**

Is any one of you in trouble? He should pray. Is anyone happy? Let him sing songs of praise. Is any one of you sick? He should call the elders of the church to pray over him and anoint him with oil in the name of the LORD. And the prayer offered in faith will make the sick person well; the LORD will raise him up. If he has sinned, he will be forgiven. Therefore confess your sins to each other and pray for each other so that you may be healed. The prayer of a righteous man is powerful and effective.

—**James 5:13–16**

Friday

Heal me, O LORD, and I will be healed;
save me and I will be saved,
for you are the one I praise.

—Jeremiah 17:14

When Jesus came into Peter's house, he saw Peter's mother-in-law lying in bed with a fever. He touched her hand and the fever left her, and she got up and began to wait on him.

When evening came, many who were demon-possessed were brought to him, and he drove out the spirits with a word and healed all the sick. This was to fulfill what was spoken through the prophet Isaiah:

"He took up our infirmities
and carried our diseases."

—Matthew 8:14–17

Weekend

When Jesus had entered Capernaum, a centurion came to him, asking for help. "LORD," he said, "my servant lies at home paralyzed and in terrible suffering." Jesus said to him, "I will go and heal him." The centurion replied, "LORD, I do not deserve to have you come under my roof. But just say the word, and my servant will be healed. For I myself am a man under authority, with soldiers under me. I tell this one, 'Go,' and he goes; and that one, 'Come,' and he comes." Jesus ... said to those following him, ... "I have not found anyone in Israel with such great faith. I say to you that many will come from the east and the west, and will take their places at the feast with Abraham, Isaac and Jacob in the kingdom of heaven. But the subjects of the kingdom will be thrown outside, into the darkness, where there will be weeping and gnashing of teeth." Then Jesus said to the centurion, "Go! It will be done just as you believed it would." And his servant was healed at that very hour.

—Matthew 8:5–13

LISTENING TO ADVICE

Monday

Now then, my sons, listen to me;
  do not turn aside from what I say.
Keep to a path far from her,
  do not go near the door of her house,
lest you give your best strength to others
  and your years to one who is cruel,
lest strangers feast on your wealth
  and your toil enrich another man's house.
At the end of your life you will groan,
  when your flesh and body are spent.
You will say, "How I hated discipline!
  How my heart spurned correction!
I would not obey my teachers
  or listen to my instructors.
I have come to the brink of utter ruin
  in the midst of the whole assembly."

—Proverbs 5:7–14

Tuesday

He who ignores discipline comes to poverty and shame,
  but whoever heeds correction is honored.

—Proverbs 13:18

He who obeys instructions guards his life,
  but he who is contemptuous of his ways
will die.

—Proverbs 19:16

Listen to advice and accept instruction,
  and in the end you will be wise.

—Proverbs 19:20

A man who remains stiff-necked after
many rebukes
  will suddenly be destroyed—without remedy.

—Proverbs 29:1

Wednesday

He who listens to a life-giving rebuke
will be at home among the wise.

—**Proverbs 15:31**

Wounds from a friend can be trusted,
but an enemy multiplies kisses.

—**Proverbs 27:6**

Perfume and incense bring joy to the heart,
and the pleasantness of one's friend springs
from his earnest counsel.

—**Proverbs 27:9**

As iron sharpens iron,
so one man sharpens another.

—**Proverbs 27:17**

LISTENING TO ADVICE

Thursday

The way of a fool seems right to him,
   but a wise man listens to advice.

—Proverbs 12:15

Stern discipline awaits him who leaves the path;
   he who hates correction will die.

Death and Destruction lie open before
the LORD—
   how much more the hearts of men!

A mocker resents correction;
   he will not consult the wise.

—Proverbs 15:10–12

For lack of guidance a nation falls,
   but many advisers make victory sure.

—Proverbs 11:14

Friday

A wise son heeds his father's instruction,
  but a mocker does not listen to rebuke.

—**Proverbs 13:1**

Pride only breeds quarrels,
  but wisdom is found in those who take advice.

—**Proverbs 13:10**

A fool spurns his father's discipline,
  but whoever heeds correction shows prudence.

—**Proverbs 15:5**

He who scorns instruction will pay for it,
  but he who respects a command is rewarded.

—**Proverbs 13:13**

Weekend

Whoever corrects a mocker invites insult;
   whoever rebukes a wicked man incurs abuse.
Do not rebuke a mocker or he will hate you;
   rebuke a wise man and he will love you.
Instruct a wise man and he will be wiser still;
   teach a righteous man and he will add to
his learning."

—Proverbs 9:7–9

He who rebukes a man will in the end gain
more favor
   than he who has a flattering tongue.

—Proverbs 28:23

Make plans by seeking advice;
   if you wage war, obtain guidance.

—Proverbs 20:18

CONTROLLING ANGER

Monday

"In your anger do not sin": Do not let the sun go
down while you are still angry.

—**Ephesians 4:26**

A gentle answer turns away wrath,
but a harsh word stirs up anger.

—**Proverbs 15:1**

The end of a matter is better than its beginning,
and patience is better than pride.
Do not be quickly provoked in your spirit,
for anger resides in the lap of fools.

—**Ecclesiastes 7:8–9**

A fool gives full vent to his anger,
but a wise man keeps himself under control.

—**Proverbs 29:11**

CONTROLLING ANGER

Tuesday

Man's anger does not bring about the righteous life that God desires. Therefore, get rid of all moral filth and the evil that is so prevalent and humbly accept the word planted in you, which can save you.

—**James 1:20–21**

Refrain from anger and turn from wrath;
  do not fret—it leads only to evil.
For evil men will be cut off,
  but those who hope in the LORD will inherit
the land.

—**Psalm 37:8–9**

Mockers stir up a city,
  but wise men turn away anger.

—**Proverbs 29:8**

A kind man benefits himself,
  but a cruel man brings trouble on himself.

—**Proverbs 11:17**

Wednesday

As charcoal to embers and as wood to fire,
so is a quarrelsome man for kindling strife.

—**Proverbs 26:21**

The LORD is compassionate and gracious,
slow to anger, abounding in love.
He will not always accuse,
nor will he harbor his anger forever;
he does not treat us as our sins deserve
or repay us according to our iniquities.
For as high as the heavens are above the earth,
so great is his love for those who fear him;
as far as the east is from the west,
so far has he removed our transgressions
from us.
As a father has compassion on his children,
so the LORD has compassion on those who
fear him.

—**Psalm 103:8–13**

CONTROLLING ANGER

Thursday

When they hurled their insults at him, he did not retaliate; when he suffered, he made no threats. Instead, he entrusted himself to him who judges justly.

—1 Peter 2:23

"If you have played the fool and
exalted yourself,
  or if you have planned evil,
  clap your hand over your mouth!
For as churning the milk produces butter,
  and as twisting the nose produces blood,
  so stirring up anger produces strife."

—Proverbs 30:32–33

" 'Do not seek revenge or bear a grudge against one of your people, but love your neighbor as yourself. I am the LORD.' "

—Leviticus 19:18

Friday

When we are slandered, we answer kindly.

—**1 Corinthians 4:13**

Do not say, "I'll do to him as he has done to me;
I'll pay that man back for what he did."

—**Proverbs 24:29**

Who is a God like you,
who pardons sin and forgives
the transgression
of the remnant of his inheritance?
You do not stay angry forever
but delight to show mercy.
You will again have compassion on us;
you will tread our sins underfoot
and hurl all our iniquities into the depths of
the sea.

—**Micah 7:18–19**

Weekend

The LORD looked with favor on Abel and his offering, but on Cain and his offering he did not look with favor. So Cain was very angry, and his face was downcast.

Then the LORD said to Cain, "Why are you angry? Why is your face downcast? If you do what is right, will you not be accepted? But if you do not do what is right, sin is crouching at your door; it desires to have you, but you must master it."

Now Cain said to his brother Abel, "Let's go out to the field." And while they were in the field, Cain attacked his brother Abel and killed him.

Then the LORD said to Cain, "Where is your brother Abel?"

"I don't know," he replied. "Am I my brother's keeper?"

The LORD said, "What have you done? Listen! Your brother's blood cries out to me from the ground. Now you are under a curse and driven from the ground, which opened its mouth to receive your brother's blood from your hand."

—Genesis 4:4–11

A GOOD REPUTATION

Monday

Good understanding wins favor,
    but the way of the unfaithful is hard.

—Proverbs 13:15

Even a child is known by his actions,
    by whether his conduct is pure and right.

—Proverbs 20:11

The boy Samuel continued to grow in stature and in favor with the LORD and with men.

—1 Samuel 2:26

[David], son of Jesse of Bethlehem ... knows how to play the harp. He is a brave man and a warrior. He speaks well and is a fine-looking man. And the LORD is with him.

—1 Samuel 16:18

Jesus grew in wisdom and stature, and in favor with God and men.

—Luke 2:52

Tuesday

The memory of the righteous will be a blessing,
but the name of the wicked will rot.

—**Proverbs 10:7**

"**Y**ou are the light of the world. A city on a hill
cannot be hidden. Neither do people light a
lamp and put it under a bowl. Instead they put it
on its stand, and it gives light to everyone in the
house. In the same way, let your light shine
before men, that they may see your good deeds
and praise your Father in heaven."

—**Matthew 5:14–16**

For you are a people holy to the LORD your God.
The LORD your God has chosen you out of all the
peoples on the face of the earth to be his people,
his treasured possession.

—**Deuteronomy 7:6**

A kindhearted woman gains respect.

—**Proverbs 11:16**

A GOOD REPUTATION

Wednesday

A man is praised according to his wisdom,
  but men with warped minds are despised.

—**Proverbs 12:8**

A dispute arose among [Jesus' disciples] as to which of them was considered to be the greatest. Jesus said to them, "The kings of the Gentiles LORD it over them; and those who exercise authority over them call themselves Benefactors. But you are not to be like that. Instead, the greatest among you should be like the youngest, and the one who rules like the one who serves. For who is greater, the one who is at the table or the one who serves? Is it not the one who is at the table? But I am among you as one who serves."

—**Luke 22:24–27**

JESUS SAID:
"He who is least among you all—he is the greatest."

—**Luke 9:48**

A GOOD REPUTATION

Thursday

At this, the administrators and the satraps tried to find grounds for charges against Daniel in his conduct of government affairs.... They could find no corruption in him, because he was trustworthy and neither corrupt nor negligent.

—**Daniel 6:4**

A *good name is more desirable than great riches;*
   to be esteemed is better than silver or gold.

—**Proverbs 22:1**

BOAZ SAID TO RUTH:
"All my fellow townsmen know that you are a *woman of noble character.*"

—**Ruth 3:11**

PAUL SAID TO TIMOTHY:
"Don't let anyone look down on you because you are young, but set an example for the believers in speech, in life, in love, in faith and in purity."

—**1 Timothy 4:12**

A GOOD REPUTATION

Friday

Do not exalt yourself in the king's presence,
    and do not claim a place among great men;
it is better for him to say to you, "Come up here,"
    than for him to humiliate you before
a nobleman.

—**Proverbs 25:6–7**

My son, do not forget my teaching,
    but keep my commands in your heart,
for they will prolong your life many years
    and bring you prosperity.

Let love and faithfulness never leave you;
bind them around your neck,
write them on the tablet of your heart.
Then you will win favor and a good name
in the sight of God and man.

—**Proverbs 3:1–4**

A GOOD REPUTATION

Weekend

A wife of noble character who can find?
　　She is worth far more than rubies.
Her husband has full confidence in her
　　and lacks nothing of value.
She brings him good, not harm,
　　all the days of her life....
Her husband is respected at the city gate,
　　where he takes his seat among the elders of
the land....
She is clothed with strength and dignity;
　　she can laugh at the days to come.
She speaks with wisdom,
　　and faithful instruction is on her tongue....
Her children arise and call her blessed;
　　her husband also, and he praises her:
Charm is deceptive, and beauty is fleeting;
　　but a woman who fears the LORD is to be
praised.

—Proverbs 31:10–12, 23, 25–26, 28, 30

Monday

A *perverse man stirs up dissension,*
and a gossip separates close friends.

—Proverbs 16:28

The good man brings good things out of the good stored up in his heart, and the evil man brings evil things out of the evil stored up in his heart. For out of the overflow of his heart his mouth speaks.

—Luke 6:45

Let your conversation be always full of grace, seasoned with salt, so that you may know how to answer everyone.

—Colossians 4:6

A *gossip betrays a confidence;*
so avoid a man who talks too much.

—Proverbs 20:19

THE PITFALLS OF GOSSIP

Tuesday

LORD, who may dwell in your sanctuary?
   Who may live on your holy hill?

He whose walk is blameless
   and who does what is righteous,
who speaks the truth from his heart
   and has no slander on his tongue,
who does his neighbor no wrong
   and casts no slur on his fellowman,
who despises a vile man
   but honors those who fear the LORD,
who keeps his oath
   even when it hurts,
who lends his money without usury
   and does not accept a bribe against
the innocent.

He who does these things
   will never be shaken.

—Psalm 15:1–5

THE PITFALLS OF GOSSIP

Wednesday

He who conceals his hatred has lying lips,
and whoever spreads slander is a fool.

—Proverbs 10:18

Without wood a fire goes out;
without gossip a quarrel dies down.

—Proverbs 26:20

He who covers over an offense promotes love,
but whoever repeats the matter separates
close friends.

—Proverbs 17:9

Do not let any unwholesome talk come out of
your mouths, but only what is helpful for building others up according to their needs, that it
may benefit those who listen.

—Ephesians 4:29

THE PITFALLS OF GOSSIP

Thursday

PAUL WRITES TO HIS FRIENDS:
I am afraid that when I come I may not find you
as I want you to be ... I fear that there may be
quarreling, jealousy, outbursts of anger, factions,
slander, gossip, arrogance and disorder.

—2 Corinthians 12:20

*With his mouth the godless destroys his
neighbor,*
   but through knowledge the righteous escape.

—Proverbs 11:9

The mouth of the righteous man utters wisdom,
   and his tongue speaks what is just.
The law of his God is in his heart;
   his feet do not slip.

—Psalm 37:30–31

THE PITFALLS OF GOSSIP

Friday

" 'Do not go about spreading slander among your people.' "

—**Leviticus 19:16**

The words of a gossip are like choice morsels;
  they go down to a man's inmost parts.

—**Proverbs 18:8**

Reckless words pierce like a sword,
  but the tongue of the wise brings healing.

—**Proverbs 12:18**

He who guards his mouth and his tongue
  keeps himself from calamity.

—**Proverbs 21:23**

Weekend

A *gossip betrays a confidence,*
but a trustworthy man keeps a secret.

—Proverbs 11:13

A *man who lacks judgment derides his neighbor,*
but a man of understanding holds
his tongue.

—Proverbs 11:12

If *you argue your case with a neighbor,*
do not betray another man's confidence,
or he who hears it may shame you
and you will never lose your bad reputation.

—Proverbs 25:9–10

A *prudent man keeps his knowledge to himself,*
but the heart of fools blurts out folly.

—Proverbs 12:23

THE PRESSURES OF CONFORMITY

Monday

Surely God is good to Israel,
    to those who are pure in heart.

But as for me, my feet had almost slipped;
    I had nearly lost my foothold.
For I envied the arrogant
    when I saw the prosperity of the wicked....
This is what the wicked are like—
    always carefree, they increase in wealth.

Surely in vain have I kept my heart pure;
    in vain have I washed my hands in innocence.
All day long I have been plagued;
    I have been punished every morning....
When I tried to understand all this,
    it was oppressive to me
till I entered the sanctuary of God;
    then I understood their final destiny.

—Psalm 73:1–3, 12–14, 16–17

Tuesday

Do not conform any longer to the pattern of this world, but be transformed by the renewing of your mind.

—**Romans 12:2**

"**Y**ou have said, 'It is futile to serve God. What did we gain by carrying out his requirements and going about like mourners before the LORD Almighty? But now we call the arrogant blessed. Certainly the evildoers prosper, and even those who challenge God escape.' "

Then those who feared the LORD talked with each other, and the LORD listened and heard. A scroll of remembrance was written in his presence concerning those who feared the LORD and honored his name.

"They will be mine," says the LORD Almighty, "in the day when I make up my treasured possession. I will spare them.... And you will again see the distinction between the righteous and the wicked, between those who serve God and those who do not."

—**Malachi 3:14–18**

THE PRESSURES OF CONFORMITY

Wednesday

Prepare your minds for action; be self-controlled; set your hope fully on the grace to be given you when Jesus Christ is revealed. As obedient children, do not conform to the evil desires you had when you lived in ignorance. But just as he who called you is holy, so be holy in all you do; for it is written: "Be holy, because I am holy."

—1 Peter 1:13–16

Peter and the other apostles replied [to the authorities]: "We must obey God rather than men!"

—Acts 5:29

The Israelites who had returned from the exile ate [the Passover], together with all who had separated themselves from the unclean practices of their Gentile neighbors in order to seek the LORD, the God of Israel.

—Ezra 6:21

THE PRESSURES OF CONFORMITY

Thursday

How can a young man keep his way pure?
  By living according to your word.
I seek you with all my heart;
  do not let me stray from your commands.
I have hidden your word in my heart
  that I might not sin against you.
Praise be to you, O LORD;
  teach me your decrees.
With my lips I recount
  all the laws that come from your mouth.
I rejoice in following your statutes
  as one rejoices in great riches.
I meditate on your precepts
  and consider your ways.
I delight in your decrees;
  I will not neglect your word.

—Psalm 119:9–16

THE PRESSURES OF CONFORMITY

Friday

"As for you, son of man, your countrymen are talking together about you by the walls and at the doors of the houses, saying to each other, 'Come and hear the message that has come from the LORD.' My people come to you, as they usually do, and sit before you to listen to your words, but they do not put them into practice. With their mouths they express devotion, but their hearts are greedy for unjust gain. Indeed, to them you are nothing more than one who sings love songs with a beautiful voice and plays an instrument well, for they hear your words but do not put them into practice."

—Ezekiel 33:30–32

You are the children of the LORD your God. Do not cut yourselves or shave the front of your heads for the dead, for you are a people holy to the LORD your God. Out of all the peoples on the face of the earth, the LORD has chosen you to be his treasured possession.

—Deuteronomy 14:1–2

THE PRESSURES OF CONFORMITY

Weekend

O LORD, *by your hand save me from
[wicked] men,*
   *from men of this world whose reward is in
this life.*

—Psalm 17:14

PAUL WRITES TO HIS FRIENDS:
Join with others in following my example, brothers, and take note of those who live according to the pattern we gave you. For, as I have often told you before and now say again even with tears, many live as enemies of the cross of Christ. Their destiny is destruction, their god is their stomach, and their glory is in their shame. Their mind is on earthly things. But our citizenship is in heaven. And we eagerly await a Savior from there, the LORD Jesus Christ, who, by the power that enables him to bring everything under his control, will transform our lowly bodies so that they will be like his glorious body.

—Philippians 3:17–21

Monday

In you, O LORD, I have taken refuge;
  let me never be put to shame;
  deliver me in your righteousness.
Turn your ear to me,
  come quickly to my rescue;
be my rock of refuge,
  a strong fortress to save me.
Since you are my rock and my fortress,
  for the sake of your name lead and guide me.
Free me from the trap that is set for me,
  for you are my refuge.
Into your hands I commit my spirit;
  redeem me, O LORD, the God of truth.

—Psalm 31:1–5

My flesh and my heart may fail,
  but God is the strength of my heart
  and my portion forever.

—Psalm 73:26

THE NEED FOR COURAGE

Tuesday

The Sovereign LORD has given me an
instructed tongue,
    to know the word that sustains the weary.
He wakens me morning by morning,
    wakens my ear to listen like one being taught.
The Sovereign LORD has opened my ears,
    and I have not been rebellious;
    I have not drawn back....
Because the Sovereign LORD helps me,
    I will not be disgraced.
Therefore have I set my face like flint,
    and I know I will not be put to shame.
He who vindicates me is near.
    Who then will bring charges against me?
    Let us face each other!
Who is my accuser?
    Let him confront me!
It is the Sovereign LORD who helps me.
    Who is he that will condemn me?

—Isaiah 50:4–5, 7–9

Wednesday

Be merciful to me, O LORD, for I am in distress;
 my eyes grow weak with sorrow,
 my soul and my body with grief.
My life is consumed by anguish
 and my years by groaning;
my strength fails because of my affliction,
 and my bones grow weak.
Because of all my enemies,
 I am the utter contempt of my neighbors;
I am a dread to my friends—
 those who see me on the street flee from me.
I am forgotten by them as though I were dead;
 I have become like broken pottery.
For I hear the slander of many;
 there is terror on every side;
they conspire against me
 and plot to take my life.

—Psalm 31:9–13

Thursday

Do not fear, for I am with you;
　do not be dismayed, for I am your God.
I will strengthen you and help you;
　I will uphold you with my righteous right hand.

All who rage against you
　will surely be ashamed and disgraced;
those who oppose you
　will be as nothing and perish.
Though you search for your enemies,
　you will not find them.
Those who wage war against you
　will be as nothing at all.
For I am the LORD, your God,
　who takes hold of your right hand
and says to you, Do not fear;
　I will help you.

—Isaiah 41:10–13

THE NEED FOR COURAGE

Friday

GOD SAID TO ISRAEL:
"Was my arm too short to ransom you?
Do I lack the strength to rescue you?
By a mere rebuke I dry up the sea,
I turn rivers into a desert;
their fish rot for lack of water
and die of thirst.
I clothe the sky with darkness
and make sackcloth its covering."

—**Isaiah 50:2–3**

This is what the LORD says to you: "Do not be afraid or discouraged because of this vast army. For the battle is not yours, but God's."

—**2 Chronicles 20:15**

THE NEED FOR COURAGE

Weekend

How great is your goodness,
which you have stored up for those who
fear you,
which you bestow in the sight of men
on those who take refuge in you.
In the shelter of your presence you hide them
from the intrigues of men;
in your dwelling you keep them safe
from accusing tongues.

Praise be to the LORD,
for he showed his wonderful love to me
when I was in a besieged city.
In my alarm I said,
"I am cut off from your sight!"
Yet you heard my cry for mercy
when I called to you for help.

—**Psalm 31:19–22**

Monday

I went past the field of the sluggard,
   past the vineyard of the man who
lacks judgment;
thorns had come up everywhere,
   the ground was covered with weeds,
   and the stone wall was in ruins.
I applied my heart to what I observed
   and learned a lesson from what I saw:
A little sleep, a little slumber,
   a little folding of the hands to rest—
and poverty will come on you like a bandit
   and scarcity like an armed man.

—**Proverbs 24:30–34**

Never be lacking in zeal, but keep your spiritual fervor, serving the LORD. Be joyful in hope, patient in affliction, faithful in prayer.

—**Romans 12:11–12**

Tuesday

The sluggard says, "There is a lion in the road,
  a fierce lion roaming the streets!"

As a door turns on its hinges,
  so a sluggard turns on his bed.

The sluggard buries his hand in the dish;
  he is too lazy to bring it back to his mouth.

The sluggard is wiser in his own eyes
  than seven men who answer discreetly.

—Proverbs 26:13–16

We want each of you to show this same diligence to the very end, in order to make your hope sure. We do not want you to become lazy, but to imitate those who through faith and patience inherit what has been promised.

—Hebrews 6:11–12

Wednesday

As vinegar to the teeth and smoke to the eyes,
so is a sluggard to those who send him.

— **Proverbs 10:26**

Diligent hands will rule,
but laziness ends in slave labor.

— **Proverbs 12:24**

Laziness brings on deep sleep,
and the shiftless man goes hungry.

— **Proverbs 19:15**

The sluggard says, "There is a lion outside!"
or, "I will be murdered in the streets!"

— **Proverbs 22:13**

The sluggard craves and gets nothing,
but the desires of the diligent are fully satisfied.

— **Proverbs 13:4**

RESISTING LAZINESS

Thursday

In the name of the LORD Jesus Christ, we command you, brothers, to keep away from every brother who is idle and does not live according to the teaching you received from us. For you yourselves know how you ought to follow our example. We were not idle when we were with you, nor did we eat anyone's food without paying for it. On the contrary, we worked night and day, laboring and toiling so that we would not be a burden to any of you. We did this, not because we do not have the right to such help, but in order to make ourselves a model for you to follow. For even when we were with you, we gave you this rule: "If a man will not work, he shall not eat." We hear that some among you are idle. They are not busy; they are busybodies. Such people we command and urge in the LORD Jesus Christ to settle down and earn the bread they eat. And as for you, brothers, never tire of doing what is right.

—2 Thessalonians 3:6–13

Friday

One who is slack in his work
  is brother to one who destroys.

—**Proverbs 18:9**

[These people] get into the habit of being idle
and going about from house to house. And not
only do they become idlers, but also gossips and
busybodies, saying things they ought not to.

—**1 Timothy 5:13**

Sow your seed in the morning,
  and at evening let not your hands be idle,
for you do not know which will succeed,
  whether this or that,
  or whether both will do equally well.

—**Ecclesiastes 11:6**

RESISTING LAZINESS

Weekend

Lazy hands make a man poor,
  but diligent hands bring wealth.

—**Proverbs 10:4**

The lazy man does not roast his game,
  but the diligent man prizes his possessions.

—**Proverbs 12:27**

If a man is lazy, the rafters sag;
  if his hands are idle, the house leaks.

—**Ecclesiastes 10:18**

The sluggard's craving will be the death of him,
  because his hands refuse to work.
All day long he craves for more,
  but the righteous give without sparing.

—**Proverbs 21:25–26**

WATCHING YOUR TEMPER

Monday

A hot-tempered man stirs up dissension,
but a patient man calms a quarrel.

—**Proverbs 15:18**

A man of knowledge uses words with restraint,
and a man of understanding is
even-tempered.

—**Proverbs 17:27**

May the words of my mouth and the medita-
tion of my heart
be pleasing in your sight,
O LORD, my Rock and my Redeemer.

—**Psalm 19:14**

A wise man fears the LORD and shuns evil,
but a fool is hotheaded and reckless.

—**Proverbs 14:16**

Tuesday

Jonah was greatly displeased [at the LORD's compassion on his enemies] and became angry. He prayed to the LORD, ... "O LORD, take away my life, for it is better for me to die than to live." But the LORD replied, "Have you any right to be angry?" Jonah went out ... and waited to see what would happen to the city [of Nineveh]. Then the LORD God provided a vine and made it grow up over Jonah to give shade for his head.... But at dawn the next day God provided a worm, which chewed the vine so that it withered. When the sun rose, God provided a scorching east wind, and the sun blazed on Jonah's head.... He wanted to die, and said, "It would be better for me to die than to live." But God said to Jonah, "Do you have a right to be angry about the vine?"..."You did not tend it or make it grow. It sprang up overnight and died overnight. But Nineveh has more than a hundred and twenty thousand people who cannot tell their right hand from their left, and many cattle as well. *Should I not be concerned about that great city?*"

—Jonah 4:1–11

Wednesday

A hot-tempered man must pay the penalty;
   if you rescue him, you will have to do it again.

—**Proverbs 19:19**

Better a patient man than a warrior,
   a man who controls his temper than one who
takes a city.

—**Proverbs 16:32**

But the fruit of the Spirit is love, joy, peace, patience, kindness, goodness, faithfulness, gentleness and self-control. Against such things there is no law. Those who belong to Christ Jesus have crucified the sinful nature with its passions and desires. Since we live by the Spirit, let us keep in step with the Spirit.

—**Galatians 5:22–25**

Your beauty ... should be that of your inner self, the unfading beauty of a gentle and quiet spirit, which is of great worth in God's sight.

—**1 Peter 3:3–4**

Thursday

Though you probe my heart and examine me
at night,
   though you test me, you will find nothing;
   I have resolved that my mouth will not sin.
As for the deeds of men—-
   by the word of your lips
I have kept myself
   from the ways of the violent.
My steps have held to your paths;
   my feet have not slipped.

I call on you, O God, for you will answer me;
   give ear to me and hear my prayer.
Show the wonder of your great love,
   you who save by your right hand
   those who take refuge in you from their foes.
Keep me as the apple of your eye;
   hide me in the shadow of your wings
from the wicked who assail me,
   from my mortal enemies who surround me.

—Psalm 17:3–9

Friday

PAUL WRITES:
Live a life worthy of the calling you have received.
Be completely humble and gentle; be patient,
bearing with one another in love. Make every
effort to keep the unity of the Spirit through the
bond of peace.

—**Ephesians 4:1–3**

Since an overseer is entrusted with God's work,
he must be blameless.... He must be hospitable,
one who loves what is good, who is self-controlled, upright, holy and disciplined. He must
hold firmly to the trustworthy message as it has
been taught, so that he can encourage others by
sound doctrine and refute those who oppose it.
For there are many rebellious people, mere talk-
ers and deceivers, especially those of the cir-
cumcision group. They must be silenced,
because they are ruining whole households by
teaching things they ought not to teach—and
that for the sake of dishonest gain.

—**Titus 1:7–11**

Weekend

A patient man has great understanding,
  but a quick-tempered man displays folly.

—**Proverbs 14:29**

Get rid of all bitterness, rage and anger, brawling and slander, along with every form of malice. Be kind and compassionate to one another, forgiving each other, just as in Christ God forgave you.

—**Ephesians 4:31–32**

A quick-tempered man does foolish things,
  and a crafty man is hated.

—**Proverbs 14:17**

A fool shows his annoyance at once,
  but a prudent man overlooks an insult.

—**Proverbs 12:16**

The heart of the righteous weighs its answers,
  but the mouth of the wicked gushes evil.

—**Proverbs 15:28**

Monday

Then Moses went up to God, and the LORD called to him from the mountain and said, "This is what you are to say to the house of Jacob and what you are to tell the people of Israel: 'You yourselves have seen what I did to Egypt, and how I carried you on eagles' wings and brought you to myself. Now if you obey me fully and keep my covenant, then out of all nations you will be my treasured possession. Although the whole earth is mine, you will be for me a kingdom of priests and a holy nation.' These are the words you are to speak to the Israelites."

So Moses went back and summoned the elders of the people and set before them all the words the LORD had commanded him to speak. The people all responded together, "We will do everything the LORD has said." So Moses brought their answer back to the LORD.

—Exodus 19:3–8

Tuesday

The Israelites did evil in the eyes of the LORD, and for seven years he gave them into the hands of the Midianites.... Midian so impoverished the Israelites that they cried out to the LORD for help. [The LORD] sent them a prophet, who said, "This is what the LORD, the God of Israel, says: ... I snatched you from the power of Egypt and from the hand of all your oppressors. I ... gave you their land. I said to you, 'I am the LORD your God; do not worship the gods of the Amorites.' ... But you have not listened to me." The angel of the LORD ... appeared to Gideon and said, "The LORD is with you, mighty warrior." "But sir," Gideon replied, "if the LORD is with us, why has all this happened to us? ... The LORD has abandoned us and put us into the hand of Midian." The LORD ... said, "Go ... save Israel out of Midian's hand." "But LORD," Gideon asked, "how can I save Israel? My clan is the weakest in Manasseh, and I am the least in my family." The LORD answered, "I will be with you, and you will strike down all the Midianites."

—Judges 6:1, 6, 8–16

Wednesday

Everyone has heard about your obedience, so I am full of joy over you; but I want you to be wise about what is good, and innocent about what is evil.

—**Romans 16:19**

"**W**hy do you call me, 'LORD, LORD,' and do not do what I say? I will show you what he is like who comes to me and hears my words and puts them into practice. He is like a man building a house, who dug down deep and laid the foundation on rock. When a flood came, the torrent struck that house but could not shake it, because it was well built. But the one who hears my words and does not put them into practice is like a man who built a house on the ground without a foundation. The moment the torrent struck that house, it collapsed and its destruction was complete."

—**Luke 6:46-49**

Thursday

"**A**braham will surely become a great and powerful nation, and all nations on earth will be blessed through him. For I have chosen him, so that he will direct his children and his household after him to keep the way of the LORD by doing what is right and just, so that the LORD will bring about for Abraham what he has promised him."

—**Genesis 18:18–19**

I have kept my feet from every evil path
  so that I might obey your word.
I have not departed from your laws,
  for you yourself have taught me.
How sweet are your words to my taste,
  sweeter than honey to my mouth!
I gain understanding from your precepts;
  therefore I hate every wrong path.

—**Psalm 119:101–104**

Friday

We know that we have come to know him if we obey his commands. The man who says, "I know him," but does not do what he commands is a liar, and the truth is not in him. But if anyone obeys his word, God's love is truly made complete in him. This is how we know we are in him: Whoever claims to live in him must walk as Jesus did.

—1 John 2:3–6

This is what the LORD says: Do what is just and right. Rescue from the hand of his oppressor the one who has been robbed. Do no wrong or violence to the alien, the fatherless or the widow, and do not shed innocent blood in this place.

—Jeremiah 22:3

The mind of sinful man is death, but the mind controlled by the Spirit is life and peace; the sinful mind is hostile to God. It does not submit to God's law, nor can it do so. Those controlled by the sinful nature cannot please God.

—Romans 8:6–8

Weekend

YOUR ATTITUDE SHOULD BE THE
SAME AS THAT OF CHRIST JESUS:
Who, being in very nature God,
   did not consider equality with God something
to be grasped,
but made himself nothing,
   taking the very nature of a servant, ...
   he humbled himself
   and became obedient to death—
      even death on a cross!
Therefore God exalted him to the highest place
   and gave him the name that is above
every name,
   that at the name of Jesus every knee
should bow,
   in heaven and on earth and under the earth,
and every tongue confess that Jesus Christ
is LORD,
   to the glory of God the Father.

—**Philippians 2:5–11**

Monday

Search me, O God, and know my heart;
   test me and know my anxious thoughts.
See if there is any offensive way in me,
   and lead me in the way everlasting.

—Psalm 139:23–24

Those who hope in the LORD
   will renew their strength.
They will soar on wings like eagles;
   they will run and not grow weary,
   they will walk and not be faint.

—Isaiah 40:31

Cast all your anxiety on [God] because he cares
for you.

—1 Peter 5:7

Blessed are those who mourn,
   for they will be comforted.

—Matthew 5:4

Tuesday

Banish anxiety from your heart
and cast off the troubles of your body.

—**Ecclesiastes 11:10**

"**P**eace, peace, to those far and near,"
said the LORD. "And I will heal them."
But the wicked are like the tossing sea,
which cannot rest,
whose waves cast up mire and mud.
"There is no peace," says my God, "for
the wicked."

—**Isaiah 57:19–21**

Do not be anxious about anything, but in everything, by prayer and petition, with thanksgiving,
present your requests to God. And the peace
of God, which transcends all understanding,
will guard your hearts and your minds in
Christ Jesus.

—**Philippians 4:6–7**

DEALING WITH ANXIETY

Wednesday

When you pass through the waters,
   I will be with you;
and when you pass through the rivers,
   they will not sweep over you.
When you walk through the fire,
   you will not be burned;
   the flames will not set you ablaze.
For I am the LORD, your God,
   the Holy One of Israel, your Savior.

—Isaiah 43:2–3

The salvation of the righteous comes from
the LORD;
   he is their stronghold in time of trouble.
The LORD helps them and delivers them;
   he delivers them from the wicked and
saves them,
   because they take refuge in him.

—Psalm 37:39–40

Thursday

JESUS SAID:

"I tell you, do not worry about your life, what you will eat or drink; or about your body, what you will wear.... Look at the birds of the air; they do not sow or reap or store away in barns, and yet your heavenly Father feeds them. Are you not much more valuable than they? "See how the lilies of the field grow. They do not labor or spin. Yet I tell you that not even Solomon in all his splendor was dressed like one of these. If that is how God clothes the grass of the field, which is here today and tomorrow is thrown into the fire, will he not much more clothe you, O you of little faith? So do not worry.... For the pagans run after all these things, and your heavenly Father knows that you need them. But seek first his kingdom and his righteousness, and all these things will be given to you as well. Therefore do not worry about tomorrow, for tomorrow will worry about itself. Each day has enough trouble of its own."

—Matthew 6:25–26, 28–34

Friday

JOHN WRITES:
"You, dear children, are from God and have overcome [the false prophets], because the one who is in you is greater than the one who is in the world."

—1 John 4:4

The LORD is my light and my salvation—
   whom shall I fear?
The LORD is the stronghold of my life—
   of whom shall I be afraid?
When evil men advance against me
   to devour my flesh,
when my enemies and my foes attack me,
   they will stumble and fall.
Though an army besiege me,
   my heart will not fear;
though war break out against me,
   even then will I be confident.

—Psalm 27:1–3

Weekend

We know that in all things God works for the good of those who love him, who have been called according to his purpose.... If God is for us, who can be against us? He who did not spare his own Son, but gave him up for us all—how will he not also, along with him, graciously give us all things? ... Who shall separate us from the love of Christ? Shall trouble or hardship or persecution or famine or nakedness or danger or sword? ... No, in all these things we are more than conquerors through him who loved us. For I am convinced that ... [nothing] in all creation, will be able to separate us from the love of God that is in Christ Jesus our LORD.

—Romans 8:28, 31–32, 35, 37–39

Who will rise up for me against the wicked?
  Who will take a stand for me against
    evildoers?...
The LORD has become my fortress,
  and my God the rock in whom I take refuge.

—Psalm 94:16, 22

SEEKING DIRECTION

Monday

[God] knows the way that I take;
  when he has tested me, I will come forth
as gold.
My feet have closely followed his steps;
  I have kept to his way without turning aside.
I have not departed from the commands of
his lips;
  I have treasured the words of his mouth
more than my daily bread.

—Job 23:10–12

A man's steps are directed by the LORD.
  How then can anyone understand his
own way?

—Proverbs 20:24

Teach me your way, O LORD,
  and I will walk in your truth;
give me an undivided heart,
  that I may fear your name.

—Psalm 86:11

Tuesday

I will instruct you and teach you in the way
you should go;
   I will counsel you and watch over you.
Do not be like the horse or the mule,
   which have no understanding
but must be controlled by bit and bridle
   or they will not come to you.
Many are the woes of the wicked,
   but the LORD's unfailing love
   surrounds the man who trusts in him.

—**Psalm 32:8–10**

Many are the plans in a man's heart,
   but it is the LORD's purpose that prevails.

—**Proverbs 19:21**

"**O** our God, ... we have no power to face this
vast army that is attacking us. We do not know
what to do, but our eyes are upon you."

—**2 Chronicles 20:12**

Wednesday

Be careful to do what the LORD your God has commanded you; do not turn aside to the right or to the left. Walk in all the way that the LORD your God has commanded you, so that you may live and prosper and prolong your days in the land that you will possess.

—Deuteronomy 5:32–33

This is what the LORD says—
   your Redeemer, the Holy One of Israel:
"I am the LORD your God,
   who teaches you what is best for you,
   who directs you in the way you should go.
If only you had paid attention to my commands,
   your peace would have been like a river,
   your righteousness like the waves of the sea.
Your descendants would have been like the sand,
   your children like its numberless grains;
their name would never be cut off
   nor destroyed from before me."

—Isaiah 48:17–19

Thursday

I know, O LORD, that a man's life is not his own;
  it is not for man to direct his steps.

—Jeremiah 10:23

As for God, his way is perfect;
  the word of the LORD is flawless.
He is a shield
  for all who take refuge in him.
For who is God besides the LORD?
  And who is the Rock except our God?
It is God who arms me with strength
  and makes my way perfect.
He makes my feet like the feet of a deer;
  he enables me to stand on the heights.
He trains my hands for battle;
  my arms can bend a bow of bronze.
You give me your shield of victory,
  and your right hand sustains me;
  you stoop down to make me great.
You broaden the path beneath me,
  so that my ankles do not turn.

—Psalm 18:30–36

Friday

Keep me safe, O God,
for in you I take refuge....

LORD, you have assigned me my portion and
my cup;
you have made my lot secure.
The boundary lines have fallen for me in pleasant places;
surely I have a delightful inheritance.

I will praise the LORD, who counsels me;
even at night my heart instructs me.
I have set the LORD always before me.
Because he is at my right hand,
I will not be shaken.

—Psalm 16:1, 5–8

In his heart a man plans his course,
but the LORD determines his steps.

—Proverbs 16:9

Weekend

O people of Zion, who live in Jerusalem, you will weep no more. How gracious he will be when you cry for help! As soon as he hears, he will answer you. Although the LORD gives you the bread of adversity and the water of affliction, your teachers will be hidden no more; with your own eyes you will see them. Whether you turn to the right or to the left, your ears will hear a voice behind you, saying, "This is the way; walk in it."

—Isaiah 30:19–21

He has showed you, O man, what is good.
    And what does the LORD require of you?
To act justly and to love mercy
    and to walk humbly with your God.

—Micah 6:8

Your word is a lamp to my feet
    and a light for my path.

—Psalm 119:105

FACING REJECTION

Monday

Sarah said to Abraham, "Get rid of that slave woman and her son, for that slave woman's son will never share in the inheritance with my son Isaac." The matter distressed Abraham greatly because it concerned his son. But God said to him, "Do not be so distressed ... Listen to whatever Sarah tells you, because it is through Isaac that your offspring will be reckoned. I will make the son of the maidservant into a nation also, because he is your offspring." Early the next morning Abraham took some food and a skin of water and gave them to Hagar. He ... sent her off with the boy [into] the desert of Beersheba. When the water in the skin was gone, she put the boy under one of the bushes. She ... sat ... about a bowshot away, for she thought, "I cannot watch the boy die." ... She began to sob.... The angel of God called to Hagar from heaven and said to her, "What is the matter, Hagar? ... God has heard the boy crying.... Take him by the hand, for I will make him into a great nation."

—Genesis 21:10–18

Tuesday

[Joseph's brothers] ... plotted [against] him....
When Joseph came to his brothers, ... they took
him and threw him into the cistern....

His brothers pulled Joseph up out of the cistern
and sold him for twenty shekels of silver to the
Ishmaelites, who took him to Egypt....

Pharaoh said to Joseph, "Since God has made
[the meaning of my dream] known to you, there
is no one so discerning and wise as you. You
shall be in charge of my palace, and all my people are to submit to your orders."

When Joseph's brothers saw that their father was
dead, they said, "What if Joseph holds a grudge
against us and pays us back for all the wrongs
we did to him?" ... His brothers then came and
threw themselves down before him.... But
Joseph said to them, "Don't be afraid.... You
intended to harm me, but God intended it for ...
the saving of many lives. So then, don't be
afraid. I will provide for you and your children."

—**Genesis 37:18, 23–24, 28; 41:39–40; 50:15–21**

Wednesday

Who has believed our message
    and to whom has the arm of the LORD
been revealed?
He grew up before him like a tender shoot,
    and like a root out of dry ground.
He had no beauty or majesty to attract us
to him,
    nothing in his appearance that we should
desire him.
He was despised and rejected by men,
    a man of sorrows, and familiar with suffering.
Like one from whom men hide their faces
    he was despised, and we esteemed him not....

He was pierced for our transgressions,
    he was crushed for our iniquities;
the punishment that brought us peace was
upon him,
    and by his wounds we are healed.
The LORD has laid on him
    the iniquity of us all.

—Isaiah 53:1–6

Thursday

When they had crucified [Jesus], they divided up his clothes by casting lots. Above his head they placed the written charge against him: THIS IS JESUS, THE KING OF THE JEWS. Two robbers were crucified with him.... Those who passed by hurled insults at him, ... saying, "You who are going to destroy the temple and build it in three days, save yourself! Come down from the cross, if you are the Son of God!"

In the same way the chief priests, the teachers of the law and the elders mocked him. "He saved others," they said, "but he can't save himself! He's the King of Israel! Let him come down now from the cross, and we will believe in him. He trusts in God. Let God rescue him now if he wants him, for he said, 'I am the Son of God.' " ...

From the sixth hour until the ninth hour darkness came over all the land. About the ninth hour Jesus cried out in a loud voice, *"Eloi, Eloi, lama sabachthani?"*—which means, *"My God, my God, why have you forsaken me?"*

—Matthew 27:35, 37–46

FACING REJECTION

Friday

For men are not cast off
  by the LORD forever.
Though he brings grief, he will show compassion,
  so great is his unfailing love.
For he does not willingly bring affliction
  or grief to the children of men.

—**Lamentations 3:31–33**

Out of the depths I cry to you, O LORD;
  O LORD, hear my voice.
Let your ears be attentive
  to my cry for mercy.

—**Psalm 130:1–2**

You who fear the LORD, praise him!
  All you descendants of Jacob, honor him!
  Revere him, all you descendants of Israel!
For he has not despised or disdained
  the suffering of the afflicted one;
he has not hidden his face from him
  but has listened to his cry for help.

—**Psalm 22:23–24**

FACING REJECTION

Weekend

O LORD, ...
All my friends
   are waiting for me to slip, saying,
"Perhaps he will be deceived;
   then we will prevail over him
   and take our revenge on him."

But the LORD is with me like a mighty warrior;
   so my persecutors will stumble and not prevail.
They will fail and be thoroughly disgraced;
   their dishonor will never be forgotten.
O LORD Almighty, you who examine
the righteous
   and probe the heart and mind,
let me see your vengeance upon them,
   for to you I have committed my cause.

Sing to the LORD!
   Give praise to the LORD!
He rescues the life of the needy
   from the hands of the wicked.

             —Jeremiah 20:7, 10–13

THE DANGER OF PRIDE

Monday

Young men, ... be submissive to those who are older. All of you, clothe yourselves with humility toward one another, because,

"God opposes the proud
but gives grace to the humble."

Humble yourselves, therefore, under God's mighty hand, that he may lift you up in due time.

—1 Peter 5:5–6

Love the LORD, all his saints!
The LORD preserves the faithful,
but the proud he pays back in full.
Be strong and take heart,
all you who hope in the LORD.

—Psalm 31:23–24

You [O LORD] save the humble
but bring low those whose eyes are haughty.

—Psalm 18:27

Tuesday

After [King] Uzziah became powerful, his pride led to his downfall. He was unfaithful to the LORD his God, and entered the temple of the LORD to burn incense on the altar of incense. Azariah the priest with eighty other courageous priests of the LORD followed him in. They confronted him and said, "It is not right for you, Uzziah, to burn incense to the LORD. That is for the priests, the descendants of Aaron, who have been consecrated to burn incense. Leave the sanctuary, for you have been unfaithful; and you will not be honored by the LORD God."

Uzziah ... became angry.... Leprosy broke out on his forehead....[the priests] hurried him out [of the temple]....

King Uzziah had leprosy until the day he died. He lived ... excluded from the temple of the LORD. Jotham his son had charge of the palace and governed the people of the land.

—**2 Chronicles 26:16–21**

THE DANGER OF PRIDE

Wednesday

"Let not the wise man boast of his wisdom
    or the strong man boast of his strength
    or the rich man boast of his riches,
but let him who boasts boast about this:
    that he understands and knows me,
that I am the LORD, who exercises kindness,
    justice and righteousness on earth,
    for in these I delight,"
                    declares the LORD.

                                    —Jeremiah 9:23–24

We do not dare to classify or compare ourselves with some who commend themselves. When they measure themselves by themselves and compare themselves with themselves, they are not wise.... But, "Let him who boasts boast in the Lord."

                                    —2 Corinthians 10:12, 17

Thursday

PAUL WRITES:
To keep me from becoming conceited ... there was given me a thorn in my flesh, a messenger of Satan, to torment me. Three times I pleaded with the LORD to take it away from me. But he said to me, "My grace is sufficient for you, for my power is made perfect in weakness." Therefore I will boast all the more gladly about my weaknesses.... I delight in weaknesses, in insults, in hardships, in persecutions, in difficulties. For when I am weak, then I am strong.

—2 Corinthians 12:7–10

Jesus said, "I praise you, Father, LORD of heaven and earth, because you have hidden these things from the wise and learned, and revealed them to little children."

—Matthew 11:25

[The LORD] mocks proud mockers
but gives grace to the humble.

—Proverbs 3:34

THE DANGER OF PRIDE

Friday

"The mirth of the wicked is brief,
   the joy of the godless lasts but a moment.
Though his pride reaches to the heavens
   and his head touches the clouds,
he will perish forever, like his own dung;
   those who have seen him will say, 'Where
is he?'
Like a dream he flies away, no more to
be found,
   banished like a vision of the night.
The eye that saw him will not see him again;
   his place will look on him no more."

—Job 20:5–9

When pride comes, then comes disgrace,
   but with humility comes wisdom.

—Proverbs 11:2

Pride goes before destruction,
   a haughty spirit before a fall.

—Proverbs 16:18

THE DANGER OF PRIDE

Weekend

"Among my people are wicked men
  who lie in wait like men who snare birds
  and like those who set traps to catch men.
Like cages full of birds,
  their houses are full of deceit;
they have become rich and powerful
  and have grown fat and sleek.
Their evil deeds have no limit;
  they do not plead the case of the fatherless to win it,
  they do not defend the rights of the poor.
Should I not punish them for this?"
  declares the LORD.

—Jeremiah 5:26–29

Do not be proud, but be willing to associate with people of low position. Do not be conceited.

—Romans 12:16

GETTING YOUR REST

Monday

My soul finds rest in God alone;
  my salvation comes from him.
He alone is my rock and my salvation;
  he is my fortress, I will never be shaken.

How long will you assault a man?
  Would all of you throw him down—
  this leaning wall, this tottering fence?
They fully intend to topple him
  from his lofty place;
  they take delight in lies.
With their mouths they bless,
  but in their hearts they curse.

Find rest, O my soul, in God alone;
  my hope comes from him.
He alone is my rock and my salvation;
  he is my fortress, I will not be shaken.
My salvation and my honor depend on God;
  he is my mighty rock, my refuge.
Trust in him at all times, O people; ...
  for God is our refuge.

—Psalm 62:1–8

Tuesday

Because so many people were coming and going that they did not even have a chance to eat, [Jesus] said to [his disciples], "Come with me by yourselves to a quiet place and get some rest." So they went away by themselves in a boat to a solitary place.

—Mark 6:31–32

The fruit of righteousness will be peace;
    the effect of righteousness will be quietness
and confidence forever.

—Isaiah 32:17

THE LORD TOLD MOSES:
"My Presence will go with you, and I will give you rest."

—Exodus 33:14

I will lie down and sleep in peace,
    for you alone, O LORD,
    make me dwell in safety.

—Psalm 4:8

Wednesday

Praise be to the LORD, to God our Savior,
  who daily bears our burdens.

—Psalm 68:19

This is what the LORD Almighty, the God of
Israel, says: "... I will refresh the weary and satisfy the faint."

—Jeremiah 31:23, 25

This is what the Sovereign LORD, the Holy One
of Israel, says:

"In repentance and rest is your salvation,
  in quietness and trust is your strength."

—Isaiah 30:15

Of making many books there is no end, and
much study wearies the body.

—Ecclesiastes 12:12

Thursday

When you went out before your people, O God,
    when you marched through the wasteland,
the earth shook,
    the heavens poured down rain,
before God, the One of Sinai,
    before God, the God of Israel.
You gave abundant showers, O God;
    you refreshed your weary inheritance.
Your people settled in it,
    and from your bounty, O God, you provided
for the poor.

—Psalm 68:7–10

The news about [Jesus] spread ... so that crowds
of people came to hear him and to be healed of
their sicknesses. But Jesus often withdrew to
lonely places and prayed.

—Luke 5:15–16

Friday

Do you not know?
　　Have you not heard?
The LORD is the everlasting God,
　　the Creator of the ends of the earth.
He will not grow tired or weary,
　　and his understanding no one can fathom.
He gives strength to the weary
　　and increases the power of the weak.

—**Isaiah 40:28–29**

My heart is not proud, O LORD,
　　my eyes are not haughty;
I do not concern myself with great matters
　　or things too wonderful for me.
But I have stilled and quieted my soul;
　　like a weaned child with its mother,
　　like a weaned child is my soul within me.

O Israel, put your hope in the LORD
　　both now and forevermore.

—**Psalm 131:1–3**

GETTING YOUR REST

Weekend

In vain you rise early
   and stay up late,
toiling for food to eat—
   for he grants sleep to those he loves.

          —Psalm 127:2

JESUS SAID:
"Come to me, all you who are weary and bur-
dened, and I will give you rest. Take my yoke upon
you and learn from me, for I am gentle and humble in heart, and you will find rest for your souls.
For my yoke is easy and my burden is light."

          —Matthew 11:28–30

I love the LORD, for he heard my voice;
   he heard my cry for mercy.
Because he turned his ear to me,
   I will call on him as long as I live....
Be at rest once more, O my soul,
   for the LORD has been good to you.

          —Psalm 116:1–2, 7

DEVELOPING HEALTHY RELATIONSHIPS

Monday

"**D**o not judge, or you too will be judged. For in the same way you judge others, you will be judged, and with the measure you use, it will be measured to you.

"Why do you look at the speck of sawdust in your brother's eye and pay no attention to the plank in your own eye? How can you say to your brother, 'Let me take the speck out of your eye,' when all the time there is a plank in your own eye? You hypocrite, first take the plank out of your own eye, and then you will see clearly to remove the speck from your brother's eye."

—Matthew 7:1–5

May the LORD make your love increase and overflow for each other and for everyone else, just as ours does for you. May he strengthen your hearts so that you will be blameless and holy in the presence of our God and Father when our LORD Jesus comes with all his holy ones.

—1 Thessalonians 3:12–13

DEVELOPING HEALTHY RELATIONSHIPS

Tuesday

Do not gloat when your enemy falls;
  when he stumbles, do not let your heart rejoice,
or the LORD will see and disapprove
  and turn his wrath away from him.

—**Proverbs 24:17–18**

This is what the LORD Almighty says: "Just as I had determined to bring disaster upon you and showed no pity when your fathers angered me," says the LORD Almighty, "so now I have determined to do good again to Jerusalem and Judah. Do not be afraid. These are the things you are to do: Speak the truth to each other, and render true and sound judgment in your courts; do not plot evil against your neighbor, and do not love to swear falsely. I hate all this," declares the LORD.

—**Zechariah 8:14–17**

Wednesday

JESUS SAID:
My command is this: Love each other as I have loved you. Greater love has no one than this, that he lay down his life for his friends....I have called you friends, for everything that I learned from my Father I have made known to you. You did not choose me, but I chose you and appointed you to go and bear fruit—fruit that will last. Then the Father will give you whatever you ask in my name.

—John 15:12–13, 15–16

Let us be self-controlled, putting on faith and love as a breastplate, and the hope of salvation as a helmet. For God did not appoint us to suffer wrath but to receive salvation through our LORD Jesus Christ. He died for us so that, whether we are awake or asleep, we may live together with him. Therefore encourage one another and build each other up, just as in fact you are doing.

—1 Thessalonians 5:8–11

DEVELOPING HEALTHY RELATIONSHIPS

Thursday

JESUS TOLD HIS DISCIPLES:
"Love your enemies, do good to those who hate you, bless those who curse you, pray for those who mistreat you. If someone strikes you on one cheek, turn to him the other also. If someone takes your cloak, do not stop him from taking your tunic. Give to everyone who asks you, and if anyone takes what belongs to you, do not demand it back. Do to others as you would have them do to you."

—Luke 6:27–31

Now that you have purified yourselves by obeying the truth so that you have sincere love for your brothers, love one another deeply, from *the heart.*

—1 Peter 1:22

DEVELOPING HEALTHY RELATIONSHIPS

Friday

PAUL WROTE TO THE CHURCH
AT ROME:
Greet Priscilla and Aquila, my fellow workers in
Christ Jesus. They risked their lives for me. Not
only I but all the churches of the Gentiles are
grateful to them.

—Romans 16:3–4

No one has ever seen God; but if we love one
another, God lives in us and his love is made
complete in us.

—1 John 4:12

Love is patient, love is kind. It does not envy, it
does not boast, it is not proud. It is not rude, it is
not self-seeking, it is not easily angered, it keeps
no record of wrongs. Love does not delight in evil
but rejoices with the truth. It always protects,
always trusts, always hopes, always perseveres.
Love never fails.

—1 Corinthians 13:4–8

Weekend

Make every effort to add to your faith goodness; and to goodness, knowledge; and to knowledge, self-control; and to self-control, perseverance; and to perseverance, godliness; and to godliness, brotherly kindness; and to brotherly kindness, love.

—**2 Peter 1:5–7**

Brothers, do not slander one another. Anyone who speaks against his brother or judges him speaks against the law and judges it. When you judge the law, you are not keeping it, but sitting in judgment on it. There is only one Lawgiver and Judge, the one who is able to save and destroy. But you—who are you to judge your neighbor?

—**James 4:11–12**

Do not withhold good from those who deserve it, when it is in your power to act.

—**Proverbs 3:27**

RESPECTING THOSE IN AUTHORITY

Monday

He who rebels against the authority [established by God] is rebelling against what God has instituted, and those who do so will bring judgment on themselves. For rulers hold no terror for those who do right, but for those who do wrong. Do you want to be free from fear of the one in authority? Then do what is right and he will commend you. For he is God's servant to do you good. But if you do wrong, be afraid, for he does not bear the sword for nothing. He is God's servant, an agent of wrath to bring punishment on the wrongdoer. Therefore, it is necessary to submit to the authorities, not only because of possible punishment but also because of conscience. This is also why you pay taxes, for the authorities are God's servants, who give their full time to governing. Give everyone what you owe him: If you owe taxes, pay taxes; if revenue, then revenue; if respect, then respect; if honor, then honor.

—Romans 13:2–7

Tuesday

SAMUEL SAYS TO SAUL:
*"Does the LORD delight in burnt offerings
and sacrifices
    as much as in obeying the voice of the LORD?
To obey is better than sacrifice,
    and to heed is better than the fat of rams.
For rebellion is like the sin of divination,
    and arrogance like the evil of idolatry."*

—1 Samuel 15:22–23

Submit to one another out of reverence for Christ.

—Ephesians 5:21

Is not wisdom found among the aged?
    Does not long life bring understanding?

—Job 12:12

RESPECTING THOSE IN AUTHORITY

Wednesday

Now we ask you, brothers, to respect those who work hard among you, who are over you in the LORD and who admonish you. Hold them in the highest regard in love because of their work.

— **1 Thessalonians 5:12–13**

Obey your leaders and submit to their authority. They keep watch over you as men who must give an account. Obey them so that their work will be a joy, not a burden, for that would be of no advantage to you.

— **Hebrews 13:17**

A wise son brings joy to his father,
  but a foolish man despises his mother.

— **Proverbs 15:20**

Thursday

Submit yourselves for the LORD's sake to every authority instituted among men: whether to the king, as the supreme authority, or to governors, who are sent by him to punish those who do wrong and to commend those who do right. For it is God's will that by doing good you should silence the ignorant talk of foolish men. Live as free men, but do not use your freedom as a cover-up for evil; live as servants of God. Show proper respect to everyone: Love the brotherhood of believers, fear God, honor the king.

—1 Peter 2:13–17

Remember your leaders, who spoke the word of God to you. Consider the outcome of their way of life and imitate their faith.

—Hebrews 13:7

Friday

[Jesus] entered Capernaum. There a centurion's servant, whom his master valued highly, was sick and about to die. The centurion heard of Jesus and sent some elders of the Jews to him, asking him to come and heal his servant.... They pleaded earnestly with [Jesus], "This man deserves to have you do this, because he loves our nation and has built our synagogue." So Jesus went with them. He was not far from the house when the centurion sent friends to say to him: "LORD, don't trouble yourself, for I do not deserve to have you come under my roof. That is why I did not even consider myself worthy to come to you. But say the word, and my servant will be healed. For I myself am a man under authority, with soldiers under me. I tell this one, 'Go,' and he goes; and that one, 'Come,' and he comes...." Turning to the crowd following him, [Jesus] said, "I tell you, I have not found such great faith even in Israel." Then the men who had been sent returned to the house and found the servant well.

—Luke 7:1–10

Weekend

Remember the days of old;
  consider the generations long past.
Ask your father and he will tell you,
  your elders, and they will explain to you.

—Deuteronomy 32:7

"Ask the former generations
  and find out what their fathers learned,
for we were born only yesterday and
know nothing,
  and our days on earth are but a shadow.
Will they not instruct you and tell you?
  Will they not bring forth words from
their understanding?"

—Job 8:8–10

Anyone who receives instruction in the word must share all good things with his instructor.

—Galatians 6:6

STRUGGLING WITH DOUBT

Monday

Now faith is being sure of what we hope for and certain of what we do not see. This is what the ancients were commended for....

Without faith it is impossible to please God, because anyone who comes to him must believe that he exists and that he rewards those who earnestly seek him.

—**Hebrews 11:1–2, 6**

Though you have not seen [Christ], you love him; and even though you do not see him now, you believe in him and are filled with an inexpressible and glorious joy, for you are receiving the goal of your faith, the salvation of your souls.

—**1 Peter 1:8–9**

We live by faith, not by sight.

—**2 Corinthians 5:7**

Tuesday

When [Jesus, Peter, James and John] came to the other disciples, they saw a large crowd around them and the teachers of the law arguing with them. As ... the people saw Jesus, they ... ran to greet him.
"What are you arguing with them about?"
he asked. A man in the crowd answered, "Teacher, I brought you my son, who is possessed by a spirit that has robbed him of speech.... I asked your disciples to drive out the spirit, but they could not."
"O unbelieving generation," Jesus replied, "how long shall I ... put up with you? Bring the boy to me."
So they brought him. When the spirit saw Jesus, it immediately threw the boy into a convulsion.... If you can do anything, take pity on us and help us." " 'If you can'?" said Jesus. "Everything is possible for him who believes." Immediately the boy's father exclaimed, "I do believe; help me overcome my unbelief!"

—**Mark 9:14–20, 22–24**

Wednesday

The LORD appeared to Abraham near the great trees of Mamre while he was sitting at the entrance to his tent in the heat of the day. Abraham looked up and saw three men standing nearby. When he saw them, he hurried from the entrance of his tent to meet them and bowed low to the ground....

"Where is your wife Sarah?" [three men] asked [Abraham].

"There, in the tent," he said.

Then the LORD [who appeared to Abraham] said, "I will surely return to you about this time next year, and Sarah your wife will have a son."

Sarah was listening at the entrance to [their] tent. ... Abraham and Sarah were already ... past the age of childbearing. So Sarah laughed to herself. ... Then the LORD said to Abraham, "Why did Sarah laugh and say, 'Will I really have a child, now that I am old?' Is anything too hard for the LORD? I will return to you at the appointed time *next year and Sarah will have a son.*"

—Genesis 18:1–2, 9–14

STRUGGLING WITH DOUBT

Thursday

Immediately Jesus made the disciples get into the boat and go on ahead of him....
During the fourth watch of the night [from the mountainside] Jesus went out to them, walking on the lake. When the disciples saw him walking on the lake, they were terrified. "It's a ghost," they said, and cried out in fear.

Jesus ... said ... "Take courage! It is I. Don't be afraid."

"LORD, if it's you," Peter replied, "tell me to come to you on the water."

"Come," he said.

Then Peter got down out of the boat, walked on the water and came toward Jesus. But when he saw the wind, he was afraid and, beginning to sink, cried out, "LORD, save me!"

Jesus ... caught him. "You of little faith," he said, "why did you doubt?"

And when they climbed into the boat, ... those who were in the boat worshiped him, saying, "Truly you are the Son of God."

—**Matthew 14:22, 25–33**

Friday

John's disciples told him about all these things [that Jesus was doing]. Calling two of them, he sent them to the LORD to ask, "Are you the one who was to come, or should we expect someone else?" When the men came to Jesus, they said, "John the Baptist sent us to you to ask, 'Are you the one who was to come, or should we expect someone else?' " At that very time Jesus cured many who had diseases, sicknesses and evil spirits, and gave sight to many who were blind. So he replied to the messengers, "Go back and report to John what you have seen and heard: The blind receive sight, the lame walk, those who have leprosy are cured, the deaf hear, the dead are raised, and the good news is preached to the poor. Blessed is the man who does not fall away on account of me."

—Luke 7:18–23

STRUGGLING WITH DOUBT

Weekend

Now Thomas (called Didymus), one of the Twelve, was not with the disciples when Jesus came. So the other disciples told him, "We have seen the LORD!"

But he said to them, "Unless I see the nail marks in his hands and put my finger where the nails were, and put my hand into his side, I will not believe it."

A week later his disciples were in the house again, and Thomas was with them. Though the doors were locked, Jesus came and stood among them and said, "Peace be with you!" Then he said to Thomas, "Put your finger here; see my hands. Reach out your hand and put it into my side. Stop doubting and believe."

Thomas said to him, "My LORD and my God!" Then Jesus told him, "Because you have seen me, you have believed; blessed are those who have not seen and yet have believed."

—**John 20:24–29**

Monday

We know that anyone born of God does not continue to sin; the one who was born of God keeps him safe, and the evil one cannot harm him. We know that we are children of God, and that the whole world is under the control of the evil one. We know also that the Son of God has come and has given us understanding, so that we may know him who is true. And we are in him who is true—even in his Son Jesus Christ. He is the true God and eternal life.
Dear children, keep yourselves from idols.

—1 John 5:18–21

Flee from sexual immorality. All other sins a man commits are outside his body, but he who sins sexually sins against his own body. Do you not know that your body is a temple of the Holy Spirit, who is in you, whom you have received from God? You are not your own; you were bought at a price. Therefore honor God with your body.

—1 Corinthians 6:18–20

STAYING PURE IN AN EVIL ENVIRONMENT

Tuesday

Potiphar put [Joseph] in charge of his household, and he entrusted to his care everything he owned. From the time he put him in charge of his household and of all that he owned, the LORD blessed the household of the Egyptian because of Joseph.... So he left in Joseph's care everything he had; with Joseph in charge, he did not concern himself with anything except the food he ate.

Now Joseph was well-built and handsome, and after a while his master's wife took notice of Joseph and said, "Come to bed with me!"

But he refused. "With me in charge," he told her, "my master does not concern himself with anything in the house; everything he owns he has entrusted to my care. No one is greater in this house than I am. My master has withheld nothing from me except you, because you are his wife. How then could I do such a wicked thing and sin against God?" And though she spoke to Joseph day after day, he refused to go to bed with her or even be with her.

—Genesis 39:4–10

Wednesday

The LORD showed me two baskets of figs placed in front of the temple of the LORD. One basket had very good figs, like those that ripen early; the other basket had very poor figs, so bad they could not be eaten.

Then the LORD asked me, "What do you see, Jeremiah?"

"Figs," I answered. "The good ones are very good, but the poor ones are so bad they cannot be eaten."

Then the word of the Lord came to me: "This is what the Lord, the God of Israel, says: 'Like these good figs, I regard as good the exiles from Judah, whom I sent away from this place to the land of the Babylonians. My eyes will watch over them for their good, and I will bring them back to this land. I will build them up and not tear them down; I will plant them and not uproot them. I will give them a heart to know me, that I am the Lord. They will be my people, and I will be their God, for they will return to me with all their heart.' "

—Jeremiah 24:1–7

STAYING PURE IN AN EVIL ENVIRONMENT

Thursday

Do not love the world or anything in the world. If anyone loves the world, the love of the Father is not in him. For everything in the world—the cravings of sinful man, the lust of his eyes and the boasting of what he has and does—comes not from the Father but from the world. The world and its desires pass away, but the man who does the will of God lives forever.

—1 John 2:15–17

Seek the LORD while he may be found;
    call on him while he is near.
Let the wicked forsake his way
    and the evil man his thoughts.
Let him turn to the LORD, and he will have mercy on him,
    and to our God, for he will freely pardon.

—Isaiah 55:6–7

Blessed are the pure in heart,
    for they will see God.

—Matthew 5:8

Friday

Dear children, do not let anyone lead you astray. He who does what is right is righteous, just as he is righteous. He who does what is sinful is of the devil.... The Son of God appeared ... to destroy the devil's work. No one who is born of God will continue to sin, because God's seed remains in him.... This is how we know who the children of God are and who the children of the devil are: Anyone who does not do what is right is not a child of God; nor is anyone who does not love his brother.

—1 John 3:7–10

The king of Egypt said to the Hebrew midwives, ... "When you help the Hebrew women in childbirth ... if it is a boy, kill him; but if it is a girl, let her live." The midwives, however, feared God and did not do what the king of Egypt had told them to do; they let the boys live....

Because the midwives feared God, he gave them families of their own.

—Exodus 1:15–17, 21

STAYING PURE IN AN EVIL ENVIRONMENT

Weekend

Flee the evil desires of youth, and pursue right-eousness, faith, love and peace, along with those who call on the LORD out of a pure heart. Don't have anything to do with foolish and stupid argu-ments.... The LORD's Servant ... must be kind to everyone, able to teach, not resentful. Those who oppose him he must gently instruct, in the hope that God will grant them repentance leading them to a knowledge of the truth, and that they will come to their senses and escape from the trap of the devil, who has taken them captive to do his will.

—2 Timothy 2:22–26

But mark this: There will be terrible times in the last days. People will be lovers of themselves, lovers of money, boastful, proud, abusive, disobe-dient to their parents, ungrateful, unholy, without love, unforgiving, slanderous, without self-con-trol, brutal, not lovers of the good, treacherous, rash, conceited, lovers of pleasure rather than lovers of God—having a form of godliness but denying its power. Have nothing to do with them.

—2 Timothy 3:1–5

FINDING SUCCESS

Monday

Some men came and told Jehoshaphat, "A vast army is coming against you...." Alarmed, Jehoshaphat resolved to inquire of the LORD, and he proclaimed a fast for all Judah. The people of Judah came together to seek help from the LORD... Jehoshaphat bowed with his face to the ground, and all the people of Judah and Jerusalem fell down in worship before the LORD.... Early in the morning they left for the Desert of Tekoa. As they set out, Jehoshaphat stood and said, "Listen to me, Judah and people of Jerusalem! Have faith in the LORD your God and you will be upheld; have faith in his prophets and you will be successful." After consulting the people, Jehoshaphat appointed men to sing to the LORD and to praise him for the splendor of his holiness....

As they began to sing and praise, the LORD set ambushes against the men of Ammon and Moab and Mount Seir who were invading Judah, and they were defeated.

—2 Chronicles 20:2-4, 18, 20-22

Tuesday

He [who delights in the law of the LORD] is like
a tree planted by streams of water,
   which yields its fruit in season
and whose leaf does not wither.
   Whatever he does prospers.

—**Psalm 1:3**

In everything he did [David] had great success,
because the LORD was with him.

—**1 Samuel 18:14**

The path of the righteous is level;
   O upright One, you make the way of the
righteous smooth.
Yes, LORD, walking in the way of your laws,
   we wait for you;
your name and renown
   are the desire of our hearts.
My soul yearns for you in the night;
   in the morning my spirit longs for you.

—**Isaiah 26:7–9**

FINDING SUCCESS

Wednesday

Whoever gives heed to instruction prospers,
and blessed is he who trusts in the LORD.

—**Proverbs 16:20**

Plans fail for lack of counsel,
but with many advisers they succeed.

—**Proverbs 15:22**

"**B**e strong and courageous, because you will
lead these people to inherit the land I swore to
their forefathers to give them.... Be careful to
obey all the law my servant Moses gave you; do
not turn from it to the right or to the left, that you
may be successful wherever you go. Do not let
this Book of the Law depart from your mouth;
meditate on it day and night, so that you may be
careful to do everything written in it. Then you
will be prosperous and successful. Have I not
commanded you? ... Do not be terrified; do not
be discouraged, for the LORD your God will be
with you wherever you go."

—**Joshua 1:6–9**

Thursday

While Joseph was there in the prison, the LORD was with him; he showed him kindness and granted him favor in the eyes of the prison warden. So the warden put Joseph in charge of all those held in the prison, and he was made responsible for all that was done there. The warden paid no attention to anything under Joseph's care, because the LORD was with Joseph and gave him success in whatever he did.

—**Genesis 39:20–23**

"**S**uccess, success to you,
and success to those who help you,
    for your God will help you."

—**1 Chronicles 12:18**

Commit to the LORD whatever you do,
    and your plans will succeed.

—**Proverbs 16:3**

Friday

Do not fret because of evil men
 or be envious of those who do wrong;
for like the grass they will soon wither,
 like green plants they will soon die away.

Trust in the LORD and do good;
 dwell in the land and enjoy safe pasture.
Delight yourself in the LORD
 and he will give you the desires of your heart.

—Psalm 37:1–4

Uzziah was sixteen years old when he became king, and he reigned in Jerusalem fifty-two years.... He did what was right in the eyes of the LORD, just as his father Amaziah had done. He sought God during the days of Zechariah, who instructed him in the fear of God. As long as he sought the LORD, God gave him success.

—2 Chronicles 26:3–5

FINDING SUCCESS

Weekend

Taste and see that the LORD is good;
 blessed is the man who takes refuge in him.
Fear the LORD, you his saints,
 for those who fear him lack nothing.
The lions may grow weak and hungry,
 but those who seek the LORD lack no
good thing.

—Psalm 34:8–10

May he give you the desire of your heart
 and make all your plans succeed.
We will shout for joy when you are victorious
 and will lift up our banners in the name of
our God.
May the LORD grant all your requests.

—Psalm 20:4–5

There is no wisdom, no insight, no plan
 that can succeed against the LORD.

—Proverbs 21:30

Monday

The rod of correction imparts wisdom,
    but a child left to himself disgraces his mother.

—**Proverbs 29:15**

When a mocker is punished, the simple
gain wisdom;
    when a wise man is instructed, he
gets knowledge.

—**Proverbs 21:11**

Turn from evil and do good;
    then you will dwell in the land forever.
For the LORD loves the just
    and will not forsake his faithful ones.

They will be protected forever,
    but the offspring of the wicked will be cut off;
the righteous will inherit the land
    and dwell in it forever.

—**Psalm 37:27–29**

Tuesday

Blessed is he
whose transgressions are forgiven,
whose sins are covered.
Blessed is the man
whose sin the LORD does not count
against him
and in whose spirit is no deceit.

When I kept silent,
my bones wasted away
through my groaning all day long.
For day and night
your hand was heavy upon me;
my strength was sapped
as in the heat of summer.

Then I acknowledged my sin to you
and did not cover up my iniquity.
I said, "I will confess
my transgressions to the LORD"—
and you forgave
the guilt of my sin.

—Psalm 32:1–5

LEARNING FROM MISTAKES

Wednesday

Whoever loves discipline loves knowledge,
but he who hates correction is stupid.

—**Proverbs 12:1**

My brothers, if one of you should wander from the truth and someone should bring him back, remember this: Whoever turns a sinner from the error of his way will save him from death and cover over a multitude of sins.

—**James 5:19–20**

There is a way that seems right to a man,
but in the end it leads to death.

—**Proverbs 14:12**

He who conceals his sins does not prosper,
but whoever confesses and renounces them finds mercy.

—**Proverbs 28:13**

Thursday

Moses took his seat to serve as judge for the people, and they stood around him from morning till evening. When his father-in-law saw [this]..., he said, ... "What you are doing is not good. You and these people who come to you will only wear yourselves out. The work is too heavy for you; you cannot handle it alone.... You must be the people's representative before God and bring their disputes to him. Teach them the decrees and laws, and show them the way to live and the duties they are to perform. But select capable men from all the people—men who fear God, trustworthy men who hate dishonest gain—and appoint them as officials over thousands, hundreds, fifties and tens. Have them serve as judges for the people at all times, but have them bring every difficult case to you; the simple cases they can decide themselves...."

Moses listened to his father-in-law and did everything he said.

—Exodus 18:13–14, 17–22, 24

LEARNING FROM MISTAKES

Friday

Flog a mocker, and the simple will
learn prudence;
   rebuke a discerning man, and he will
gain knowledge.

—Proverbs 19:25

   "**Y**ou disciplined me like an unruly calf,
   and I have been disciplined.
Restore me, and I will return,
   because you are the LORD my God.
After I strayed,
   I repented;
after I came to understand."

—Jeremiah 31:18–19

Those who sow in tears
   will reap with songs of joy.
He who goes out weeping,
   carrying seed to sow,
will return with songs of joy,
   carrying sheaves with him.

—Psalm 126:5–6

Weekend

Good and upright is the LORD;
  therefore he instructs sinners in his ways.
He guides the humble in what is right
  and teaches them his way.
All the ways of the LORD are loving and faithful
  for those who keep the demands of
his covenant.
For the sake of your name, O LORD,
  forgive my iniquity, though it is great.
Who, then, is the man that fears the LORD?
  He will instruct him in the way chosen
for him.
He will spend his days in prosperity,
  and his descendants will inherit the land.
The LORD confides in those who fear him;
  he makes his covenant known to them.
My eyes are ever on the LORD,
  for only he will release my feet from
the snare.

—Psalm 25:8–15

GUARDING AGAINST PEER PRESSURE

Monday

Dear friends, I urge you, ... to abstain from sinful desires, which war against your soul.

—1 Peter 2:11

The wicked plot against the righteous
and gnash their teeth at them;
but the LORD laughs at the wicked,
for he knows their day is coming.
The wicked draw the sword
and bend the bow
to bring down the poor and needy,
to slay those whose ways are upright.
But their swords will pierce their own hearts,
and their bows will be broken.

Better the little that the righteous have
than the wealth of many wicked;
for the power of the wicked will be broken,
but the LORD upholds the righteous.

—Psalm 37:12–17

GUARDING AGAINST PEER PRESSURE

Tuesday

"**Be** very strong; be careful to obey all that is written in the Book of the Law of Moses, without turning aside to the right or to the left. Do not associate with these nations that remain among you; do not invoke the names of their gods or swear by them. You must not serve them or bow down to them. But you are to hold fast to the LORD your God, as you have until now."

—Joshua 23:6–8

THE ISRAELITES SAID TO SAMUEL:
"Appoint a king to lead us, such as all the other nations have."...

This displeased Samuel; so he prayed to the LORD. And the LORD told him: "... It is not you they have rejected, but they have rejected me as their king."

But the people refused to listen to Samuel. "No!" they said. "We want a king over us. Then we will be like all the other nations, with a king to lead us and to go out before us and fight our battles."

—1 Samuel 8:5–7, 19–20

GUARDING AGAINST PEER PRESSURE

Wednesday

Do not be overawed when a man grows rich,
    when the splendor of his house increases;
for he will take nothing with him when he dies,
    his splendor will not descend with him.
Though while he lived he counted
himself blessed—
    and men praise you when you prosper—
he will join the generation of his fathers,
    who will never see the light of life.
A man who has riches without understanding
    is like the beasts that perish.

—Psalm 49:16–20

If your very own brother, or your son or daughter, or the wife you love, or your closest friend secretly entices you, saying, "Let us go and worship other gods" (gods that neither you nor your fathers have known, gods of the peoples around you, whether near or far, from one end of the land to the other), do not yield to him or listen to him. Show him no pity. Do not spare him or shield him.

—Deuteronomy 13:6–8

GUARDING AGAINST PEER PRESSURE

Thursday

Nebuchadnezzar ... ordered Ashpenaz, chief of his court officials, to bring in some of the Israelites from the royal family and the nobility—young men ... qualified to serve in the king's palace.... The king assigned them a daily amount of food and wine from the king's table. They were to be trained for three years, and after that they were to enter the king's service.... But Daniel ... asked the chief official for permission not to defile himself [with the royal food and wine].... but the official told Daniel, "Why should [the King] see you looking worse than the other young men your age? The king would then have my head because of you." Daniel then said to the guard ... "Please test your servants for ten days: Give us nothing but vegetables to eat and water to drink. Then compare our appearance with that of the young men who eat the royal food, and treat your servants in accordance with what you see." So he agreed.... At the end of the ten days they looked healthier and better nourished than any of the young men who ate the royal food.

—Daniel 1:1, 3–5, 8, 10–15

GUARDING AGAINST PEER PRESSURE

Friday

Have mercy on me, O God, have mercy on me,
    for in you my soul takes refuge.
I will take refuge in the shadow of your wings
    until the disaster has passed.

I cry out to God Most High,
    to God, who fulfills his purpose for me.
He sends from heaven and saves me,
    rebuking those who hotly pursue me;
God sends his love and his faithfulness.

I am in the midst of lions;
    I lie among ravenous beasts—
men whose teeth are spears and arrows,
    whose tongues are sharp swords....
They spread a net for my feet—
    I was bowed down in distress.
They dug a pit in my path—
    but they have fallen into it themselves.

My heart is steadfast, O God,
my heart is steadfast.

—**Psalm 57:1–4, 6–7**

GUARDING AGAINST PEER PRESSURE

Weekend

Do not be yoked together with unbelievers. For what do righteousness and wickedness have in common? Or what fellowship can light have with darkness? What harmony is there between Christ and Belial? What does a believer have in common with an unbeliever? What agreement is there between the temple of God and idols? For we are the temple of the living God. As God has said: "I will live with them and walk among them, and I will be their God, and they will be my people."

"Therefore come out from them
   and be separate,
                  says the LORD.
Touch no unclean thing,
   and I will receive you."
"I will be a Father to you,
   and you will be my sons and daughters,
                  says the LORD Almighty."

—2 Corinthians 6:14–18

Monday

King Solomon asked God,
"Give me wisdom and knowledge, that I may
lead this people, for who is able to govern this
great people of yours?"
God said to Solomon, "Since this is your
heart's desire ... wisdom and knowledge will be
given you."

—2 Chronicles 1:10–12

God gave Solomon wisdom and very great
insight, and a breadth of understanding as
measureless as the sand on the seashore.... He
was wiser than any other man, including Ethan
the Ezrahite—wiser than Heman, Calcol and
Darda, the sons of Mahol.... He spoke three
thousand proverbs and his songs numbered a
thousand and five. He described plant life, from
the cedar of Lebanon to the hyssop that grows
out of walls.... Men of all nations came to listen
to Solomon's wisdom, sent by all the kings of the
world, who had heard of his wisdom.

—1 Kings 4:29, 31–34

Tuesday

I write these things to you who believe in the name of the Son of God so that you may know that you have eternal life. This is the confidence we have in approaching God: that if we ask anything according to his will, he hears us. And if we know that he hears us—whatever we ask—we know that we have what we asked of him.

—1 John 5:13–15

The LORD is with you when you are with him. If you seek him, he will be found by you.

—2 Chronicles 15:2

Let everyone who is godly pray to you
 while you may be found;
surely when the mighty waters rise,
 they will not reach him.
You are my hiding place;
 you will protect me from trouble
 and surround me with songs of deliverance.

—Psalm 32:6–7

Wednesday

"**A**sk and it will be given to you; seek and you will find; knock and the door will be opened to you. For everyone who asks receives; he who seeks finds; and to him who knocks, the door will be opened.

"Which of you, if his son asks for bread, will give him a stone? Or if he asks for a fish, will give him a snake? If you, then, though you are evil, know how to give good gifts to your children, how much more will your Father in heaven give good gifts to those who ask him!"

—Matthew 7:7–11

The heart of the discerning acquires knowledge;
   the ears of the wise seek it out.

—Proverbs 18:15

"**Y**ou will seek me and find me when you seek me with all your heart. I will be found by you," declares the LORD.

—Jeremiah 29:13–14

ASKING GOD FOR HELP

Thursday

Do not withhold your mercy from me, O LORD;
　may your love and your truth always
protect me.
For troubles without number surround me;
　my sins have overtaken me, and I cannot see.
They are more than the hairs of my head,
　and my heart fails within me.

Be pleased, O LORD, to save me;
　O LORD, come quickly to help me.
May all who seek to take my life
　be put to shame and confusion;
may all who desire my ruin
　be turned back in disgrace.
May those who say to me, "Aha! Aha!"
　be appalled at their own shame.
But may all who seek you
　rejoice and be glad in you;
may those who love your salvation always say,
　"The LORD be exalted!"...
You are my help and my deliverer;
　O my God, do not delay.

—Psalm 40:11-17

Friday

I am always with you;
   you hold me by my right hand.
You guide me with your counsel,
   and afterward you will take me into glory.
Whom have I in heaven but you?
   And earth has nothing I desire besides you.

—Psalm 73:23–25

He who trusts in himself is a fool,
   but he who walks in wisdom is kept safe.

—Proverbs 28:26

Blessed are those who hunger and thirst
for righteousness,
   for they will be filled.

—Matthew 5:6

ASKING GOD FOR HELP

Weekend

DANIEL PRAYED:
"I thank and praise you, O God of my fathers:
   You have given me wisdom and power,
you have made known to me what we asked
of you,
   you have made known to us the dream of
the king."

—Daniel 2:23

Hear, O LORD, and answer me,
   for I am poor and needy.
Guard my life, for I am devoted to you.
   You are my God; save your servant
   who trusts in you.
Have mercy on me, O LORD,
   for I call to you all day long.
Bring joy to your servant,
   for to you, O LORD,
   I lift up my soul.

—Psalm 86:1–4

Monday

We do not lose heart. Though outwardly we are wasting away, yet inwardly we are being renewed day by day. For our light and momentary troubles are achieving for us an eternal glory that far outweighs them all. So we fix our eyes not on what is seen, but on what is unseen. For what is seen is temporary, but what is unseen is eternal.

—2 Corinthians 4:16–18

Commit your way to the LORD;
*   trust in him and he will do this:*
He will make your righteousness shine like
the dawn,
the justice of your cause like the noonday sun.

Be still before the LORD and wait patiently
for him;
*   do not fret when men succeed in their ways,*
*   when they carry out their wicked schemes.*

—Psalm 37:5–7

Tuesday

How many are your works, O LORD!
In wisdom you made them all;
the earth is full of your creatures.
There is the sea, vast and spacious,
teeming with creatures beyond number—
living things both large and small.
There the ships go to and fro,
and the leviathan, which you formed to
frolic there.
These all look to you
to give them their food at the proper time.
When you give it to them,
they gather it up;
when you open your hand,
they are satisfied with good things.
When you hide your face,
they are terrified;
when you take away their breath,
they die and return to the dust.
When you send your Spirit,
they are created,
and you renew the face of the earth.

—**Psalm 104:24–30**

Wednesday

Because of the LORD's great love we are
not consumed,
    for his compassions never fail.
They are new every morning;
    great is your faithfulness.
I say to myself, "The LORD is my portion;
    therefore I will wait for him."

The LORD is good to those whose hope is in him,
    to the one who seeks him;
it is good to wait quietly
    for the salvation of the LORD.

—**Lamentations 3:22–26**

Why are you downcast, O my soul?
    Why so disturbed within me?
Put your hope in God,
    for I will yet praise him,
    my Savior and my God.

—**Psalm 42:11**

Thursday

[The LORD] makes me lie down in
green pastures,
he leads me beside quiet waters,
    he restores my soul.
He guides me in paths of righteousness
    for his name's sake.
Even though I walk
    through the valley of the shadow of death,
I will fear no evil,
    for you are with me;
your rod and your staff,
    they comfort me.

You prepare a table before me
    in the presence of my enemies.
You anoint my head with oil;
    my cup overflows.
Surely goodness and love will follow me
    all the days of my life,
and I will dwell in the house of the
LORD forever.

—Psalm 23:2–6

Friday

To you, O LORD, I lift up my soul;
    in you I trust, O my God.
Do not let me be put to shame,
    nor let my enemies triumph over me.
No one whose hope is in you
    will ever be put to shame,
but they will be put to shame
    who are treacherous without excuse.

Show me your ways, O LORD,
    teach me your paths;
guide me in your truth and teach me,
    for you are God my Savior,
    and my hope is in you all day long.

—**Psalm 25:1–5**

Though you have made me see troubles,
many and bitter,
    you will restore my life again;
from the depths of the earth
    you will again bring me up.

—**Psalm 71:20**

RENEWING YOUR SPIRIT

Weekend

Have mercy on me, O God,
  according to your unfailing love;
according to your great compassion
  blot out my transgressions.
Wash away all my iniquity
  and cleanse me from my sin....
Cleanse me with hyssop, and I will be clean;
  wash me, and I will be whiter than snow.
Let me hear joy and gladness;
  let the bones you have crushed rejoice.
Hide your face from my sins
  and blot out all my iniquity.

Create in me a pure heart, O God,
  and renew a steadfast spirit within me.
Do not cast me from your presence
  or take your Holy Spirit from me.
Restore to me the joy of your salvation
  and grant me a willing spirit, to sustain me.

—Psalm 51:1–2, 7–12

Monday

There is a time for everything,
   and a season for every activity under heaven:

   a time to be born and a time to die,
   a time to plant and a time to uproot,
   a time to kill and a time to heal,
   a time to tear down and a time to build,
   a time to weep and a time to laugh,
   a time to mourn and a time to dance,
   a time to scatter stones and a time to
gather them,
   a time to embrace and a time to refrain,
   a time to search and a time to give up,
   a time to keep and a time to throw away,
   a time to tear and a time to mend,
   a time to be silent and a time to speak,
   a time to love and a time to hate,
   a time for war and a time for peace.

—Ecclesiastes 3:1–8

Tuesday

"The fear of the LORD is the beginning
of wisdom,
   and knowledge of the Holy One
is understanding.
For through me your days will be many,
   and years will be added to your life."

—**Proverbs 9:10–11**

A man may have a hundred children and live
many years; yet no matter how long he lives, if
he cannot enjoy his prosperity and does not
receive proper burial, I say that a stillborn child
is better off than he. It comes without meaning, it
departs in darkness, and in darkness its name is
shrouded. Though it never saw the sun or knew
anything, it has more rest than does that man—
even if he lives a thousand years twice over but
fails to enjoy his prosperity. Do not all go to the
same place?

—**Ecclesiastes 6:3–6**

Wednesday

O LORD, the king rejoices in your strength.
   How great is his joy in the victories you give!
You have granted him the desire of his heart
   and have not withheld the request of his lips.

You welcomed him with rich blessings
   and placed a crown of pure gold on his head.
He asked you for life, and you gave it to him—
   length of days, for ever and ever.

—Psalm 21:1–4

Whoever obeys [the king's] command will
come to no harm,
   and the wise heart will know the proper time
and procedure.
For there is a proper time and procedure for
every matter.

—Ecclesiastes 8:5–6

God is our God for ever and ever;
   he will be our guide even to the end.

—Psalm 48:14

Thursday

Fix these words of mine in your hearts and minds; tie them as symbols on your hands and bind them on your foreheads. Teach them to your children, talking about them when you sit at home and when you walk along the road, when you lie down and when you get up. Write them on the doorframes of your houses and on your gates, so that your days and the days of your children may be many in the land that the LORD swore to give your forefathers, as many as the days that the heavens are above the earth.

—**Deuteronomy 11:18–21**

O LORD, what is man that you care for him,
the son of man that you think of him?
Man is like a breath;
his days are like a fleeting shadow.

—**Psalm 144:3–4**

Friday

"Show me, O LORD, my life's end
    and the number of my days;
    let me know how fleeting is my life.
You have made my days a mere handbreadth;
    the span of my years is as nothing before you.
    Each man's life is but a breath.
Man is a mere phantom as he goes to and fro:
    He bustles about, but only in vain;
    he heaps up wealth, not knowing who will
get it.

"But now, LORD, what do I look for?
    My hope is in you."

—**Psalm 39:4–7**

Weekend

You turn men back to dust [O LORD],
   saying, "Return to dust, O sons of men."
For a thousand years in your sight
   are like a day that has just gone by,
   or like a watch in the night.
You sweep men away in the sleep of death;
   they are like the new grass of the morning—
though in the morning it springs up new,
   by evening it is dry and withered.

We are consumed by your anger
   and terrified by your indignation.
You have set our iniquities before you,
   our secret sins in the light of your presence.
All our days pass away under your wrath;
   we finish our years with a moan.
The length of our days is seventy years—
   or eighty, if we have the strength;
yet their span is but trouble and sorrow,
   for they quickly pass, and we fly away.
Teach us to number our days aright,
   that we may gain a heart of wisdom.

—Psalm 90:3–10, 12

STRENGTH FROM GOD

Monday

I waited patiently for the LORD;
    he turned to me and heard my cry.
He lifted me out of the slimy pit,
    out of the mud and mire;
he set my feet on a rock
    and gave me a firm place to stand.
He put a new song in my mouth,
    a hymn of praise to our God.
Many will see and fear
    and put their trust in the LORD.

Blessed is the man
    who makes the LORD his trust,
who does not look to the proud,
    to those who turn aside to false gods.
Many, O LORD my God,
    are the wonders you have done.
The things you planned for us
    no one can recount to you;
were I to speak and tell of them,
    they would be too many to declare.

—Psalm 40:1–5

STRENGTH FROM GOD

Tuesday

I lift up my eyes to the hills—
    where does my help come from?
My help comes from the LORD,
    the Maker of heaven and earth.

He will not let your foot slip—
    he who watches over you will not slumber;
indeed, he who watches over Israel
    will neither slumber nor sleep.

The LORD watches over you—
    the LORD is your shade at your right hand;
the sun will not harm you by day,
    nor the moon by night.

The LORD will keep you from all harm—
    he will watch over your life;
the LORD will watch over your coming
and going
    both now and forevermore.

                     —Psalm 121:1–8

STRENGTH FROM GOD

Wednesday

But you, O Sovereign LORD,
  deal well with me for your name's sake;
  out of the goodness of your love, deliver me.
For I am poor and needy,
  and my heart is wounded within me.
I fade away like an evening shadow;
  I am shaken off like a locust.
My knees give way from fasting;
  my body is thin and gaunt.
I am an object of scorn to my accusers;
  when they see me, they shake their heads.

Help me, O LORD my God;
save me in accordance with your love.

—Psalm 109:21–26

Thursday

The LORD is my rock, my fortress and
my deliverer;

> my God is my rock, in whom I take refuge.
> He is my shield and the horn of my salvation,
> my stronghold.
> I call to the LORD, who is worthy of praise,
> and I am saved from my enemies.

The cords of death entangled me;
> the torrents of destruction overwhelmed me.
The cords of the grave coiled around me;
> the snares of death confronted me.
In my distress I called to the LORD;
> I cried to my God for help.
From his temple he heard my voice;
> my cry came before him, into his ears....
He reached down from on high and took hold
of me;
> he drew me out of deep waters.
He brought me out into a spacious place;
> he rescued me because he delighted in me.

—Psalm 18:2–6, 16, 19

Friday

Hear my voice when I call, O LORD;
　be merciful to me and answer me.
My heart says of you, "Seek his face!"
　Your face, LORD, I will seek.
Do not hide your face from me,
　do not turn your servant away in anger;
　you have been my helper.
Do not reject me or forsake me,
　O God my Savior.

Though my father and mother forsake me,
　the LORD will receive me.
Teach me your way, O LORD;
　lead me in a straight path
　because of my oppressors.

—Psalm 27:7-11

The LORD is good,
　a refuge in times of trouble.
He cares for those who trust in him.

—Nahum 1:7

STRENGTH FROM GOD

Weekend

Sing to God, O kingdoms of the earth,
   sing praise to the LORD,
to him who rides the ancient skies above,
   who thunders with mighty voice.
Proclaim the power of God,
   whose majesty is over Israel,
   whose power is in the skies.
You are awesome, O God, in your sanctuary;
   the God of Israel gives power and strength to
his people.

—Psalm 68:32–35

David sang to the LORD:
"As for God, his way is perfect;
   the word of the LORD is flawless.
He is a shield
   for all who take refuge in him.
For who is God besides the LORD?
   And who is the Rock except our God?
It is God who arms me with strength
   and makes my way perfect.

—2 Samuel 22:31–33

THE VALUE OF WISDOM

Monday

If you are wise, your wisdom will reward you;
  if you are a mocker, you alone will suffer.

—Proverbs 9:12

A wise son brings joy to his father,
  but a foolish son grief to his mother.

—Proverbs 10:1

Take heed, you senseless ones among
the people;
  you fools, when will you become wise?
Does he who implanted the ear not hear?
  Does he who formed the eye not see?
Does he who disciplines nations not punish?
  Does he who teaches man lack knowledge?
The LORD knows the thoughts of man;
  he knows that they are futile.

—Psalm 94:8–11

Tuesday

Who is wise and understanding among you? Let him show it by his good life, by deeds done in the humility that comes from wisdom. But if you harbor bitter envy and selfish ambition in your hearts, do not boast about it or deny the truth. Such "wisdom" does not come down from heaven but is earthly, unspiritual, of the devil. For where you have envy and selfish ambition, there you find disorder and every evil practice.
But the wisdom that comes from heaven is first of all pure; then peace-loving, considerate, submissive, full of mercy and good fruit, impartial and sincere. Peacemakers who sow in peace raise a harvest of righteousness.

—**James 3:13–18**

Wise men store up knowledge,
  but the mouth of a fool invites ruin.

—**Proverbs 10:14**

Wednesday

"**W**here can wisdom be found?
  Where does understanding dwell?
Man does not comprehend its worth;
  it cannot be found in the land of the living.
The deep says, 'It is not in me';
  the sea says, 'It is not with me.'
It cannot be bought with the finest gold,
  nor can its price be weighed in silver.
It cannot be bought with the gold of Ophir,
  with precious onyx or sapphires.
Neither gold nor crystal can compare with it,
  nor can it be had for jewels of gold.
Coral and jasper are not worthy of mention;
  the price of wisdom is beyond rubies.
The topaz of Cush cannot compare with it;
  it cannot be bought with pure gold."

—Job 28:12–19

Thursday

Wisdom, like an inheritance, is a good thing
  and benefits those who see the sun.
Wisdom is a shelter
  as money is a shelter,
but the advantage of knowledge is this:
  that wisdom preserves the life of its possessor.

—Ecclesiastes 7:11–12

Who is like the wise man?
  Who knows the explanation of things?
Wisdom brightens a man's face
  and changes its hard appearance.

—Ecclesiastes 8:1

The wisdom of the prudent is to give thought to
their ways,
  but the folly of fools is deception.

—Proverbs 14:8

THE VALUE OF WISDOM

Friday

"For my thoughts are not your thoughts,
   neither are your ways my ways,"
         declares the LORD.
"As the heavens are higher than the earth,
   so are my ways higher than your ways
   and my thoughts than your thoughts.
As the rain and the snow
   come down from heaven,
and do not return to it
   without watering the earth
and making it bud and flourish,
   so that it yields seed for the sower and bread
for the eater,
so is my word that goes out from my mouth:
   It will not return to me empty,
but will accomplish what I desire
   and achieve the purpose for which I sent it."

                              —Isaiah 55:8–11

THE VALUE OF WISDOM

Weekend

There was once a small city with only a few people in it. And a powerful king came against it, surrounded it and built huge siegeworks against it. Now there lived in that city a man poor but wise, and he saved the city by his wisdom. But nobody remembered that poor man. So I said, "Wisdom is better than strength."

—**Ecclesiastes 9:13–16**

Oh, the depth of the riches of the wisdom and knowledge of God!
    How unsearchable his judgments,
    and his paths beyond tracing out!
"Who has known the mind of the LORD?
    Or who has been his counselor?"
"Who has ever given to God,
    that God should repay him?"
For from him and through him and to him are all things.
    To him be the glory forever! Amen.

—**Romans 11:33–36**

At Inspirio, we love to hear from you—your
stories, your feedback,
and your product ideas.
Please send your comments to us
by way of email at
icares@zondervan.com
or to the address below:

inspirio

Attn: Inspirio Cares
5300 Patterson Avenue SE
Grand Rapids, MI 49530

If you would like further information
about Inspirio and the products we
create, please visit us at:
www.inspiriogifts.com

Thank you and God bless!